BRAIN QUEST

GRADE 2
WORKBOOK

Written by Liane Onish
Consulting Editor: Jill Swann

Workman Publishing • New York

This book belongs to:

First

Last

ISBN 978-1-5235-1736-7

New and updated text by Jen Agresta and Jennifer Szymanski; educational review by Anne Haywood, Rebecca Keller, and Peg Keiner

Illustrations by George Ulrich, Kimble Mead, Emily Bolam, Jamie Smith, and Scott Dubar, with cover illustrations by Edison Yan

Workbook series design by Raquel Jaramillo

30th Anniversary Edition Revision produced for Workman by WonderLab Group, LLC, and Fan Works Design, LLC.

Workman books are available at special discounts when purchased in bulk for premiums and sales promotions as well as for fundraising or educational use. Special editions or book excerpts can also be created to specification. For details, please contact special.markets@hbgusa.com.

WORKMAN, BRAIN QUEST, and IT'S FUN TO BE SMART! are registered trademarks of Workman Publishing Co., Inc., a subsidiary of Hachette Book Group, Inc.

Workman Publishing Co., Inc., a subsidiary of Hachette Book Group, Inc.
1290 Avenue of the Americas
New York, NY 10104
workman.com • brainquest.com

Distributed in Europe by Hachette Livre, 58 rue Jean Bleuzen, 92 178 Vanves Cedex, France.

Distributed in the United Kingdom by Hachette Book Group, UK, Carmelite House, 50 Victoria Embankment, London EC4Y 0DZ.

Printed in China on responsibly sourced paper.

First printing April 2023
10 9 8 7 6 5 4 3 2 1

Dear Parents and Caregivers,

Learning is an adventure—a quest for knowledge. At Brain Quest, we strive to guide children on that quest, to keep them motivated and curious, and to give them the confidence they need to do well in school and beyond. We're excited to partner with you and your child on this step of their lifelong knowledge quest.

BRAIN QUEST WORKBOOKS are designed to enrich children's understandings in all content areas by reinforcing the basics and previewing future learning. These are not textbooks, but rather true workbooks, and are best used to reinforce curricular concepts learned at school. Each workbook aligns with national and state learning standards and is written in consultation with an award-winning grade-level teacher.

In second grade, children build on previously learned phonics and vocabulary skills to become independent readers and writers. They expand their addition and subtraction skills and their knowledge of fractions, geometry, time, and money. Second graders also develop a greater understanding of how the world works by studying science, social studies, and technology.

We're excited that BRAIN QUEST WORKBOOKS will play an integral role in your child's educational adventure. So, let the learning—and the fun—begin!

It's fun to be smart!®

—The editors of Brain Quest

HOW TO USE THIS BOOK

Welcome to the Brain Quest Grade 2 Workbook!

Encourage your child to complete the workbook at their own pace. Guide them to approach the work with a **growth mindset**, the idea that our abilities can change and grow with effort. Reinforce this by praising effort and problem-solving and explaining that mistakes are part of learning.

The **opening page** of each section has a note for parents and caregivers and another note just for kids.

Notes for children give learners a preview of each section.

Notes for parents highlight key skills and give suggestions for helping with each section.

Guide your child to place a sticker here to get excited about learning.

35

SPELLING AND VOCABULARY

Shhh—can you find the silent letter in the word g–h–o–s–t? Don't let a hard word like *ghost* spook you! Studying spelling and vocabulary makes learning new words less of a trick and more of a treat.

PARENTS In this section, children build on the phonics skills they practiced earlier and expand their understanding of how letters combine to form short and long vowel sounds. Children also grow their vocabulary through explorations of antonyms, synonyms, homophones, and plurals.

For additional resources, visit www.BrainQuest.com/grade2

Read the directions aloud if needed. Encourage your child to work as independently as possible.

Get your child talking! Ask about the images they see and connections between the workbook and their lives.

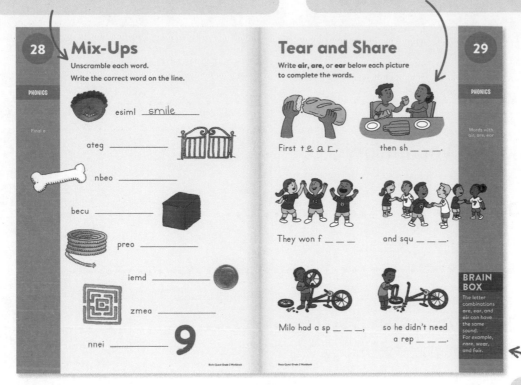

Brain Boxes offer friendly explanations of key concepts.

Cut out the Brain Quest **Mini-Deck** from the back to play and learn on the go!

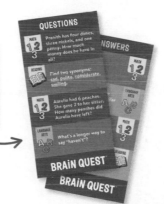

After each chapter, have your child place a sticker on the **progress map** to mark their achievement.

Encourage your child to use stickers to decorate their **certificate.** Hang it up when it's complete!

CONTENTS

PHONICS

Did you know that letter sounds can be hard or soft and long or short? Let's explore the different sounds letters make in words.

PARENTS Systematic phonics instruction improves young readers' word recognition, spelling, and reading comprehension. Learning common consonant blends and vowel combinations will help your child become a more proficient reader and writer. Remind them to use these skills to sound out unknown words.

PLACE A STICKER HERE

For additional resources, visit www.BrainQuest.com/grade2

Beginning Letters

Say the word for each picture.

What **beginning sound** do you hear?

Write the letter.

d og

__ eaf

__ ap

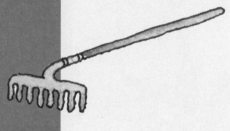

__ ake

__ arrot

__ an

__ est

6

__ ix

__ ar

__ ear

__ ite

__ ie

Ending Letters

Say the word for each picture.

What **ending sound** do you hear?

Write the letter.

 scar f

 fro __

 cu __

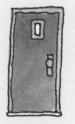 doo __

 sea __

 ca __

 su __

 be __

 eigh __

 bu __

These words end in **ss** or **ll**. What ending sound do
you hear? Write the two letters.

 be___

 dre___

 do___

It Takes Two

Say the word for each picture.

What beginning sound do you hear?

Find the correct **blend** in the boxes. Write it on the line.

bl	br	cl	cr
dr	fl	fr	gl
gr	pl	pr	sc
sl	sk	sm	sp
	st	sw	tr

p r esent

__ __ ippers

__ __ oon

__ __ apes

__ __ amp

__ __ uck

__ __ ing

__ __ ower

__ __ um

BRAIN BOX

Blends are two consonants that go together. You can hear both letters in a blend.

Example: plate

The blend in this word is **p-l**. When you say **plate**, you can hear both the **p** and **l** sounds.

_ _ ee

_ _ is

_ _ asses

_ _ ead

_ _ ool

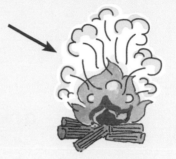

_ _ oke

_ _ ab

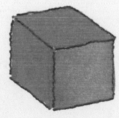

_ _ ock

_ _ ale

_ _ og

_ _ ant

_ _ ock

Shh! Sounds

Complete each word with a **digraph** from the boxes.

Draw a line from the word to its picture.

ch	sh
th	wh

<u>w</u> <u>h</u> eel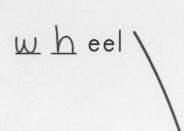

__ __ ark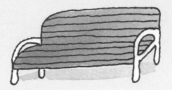

ben __ __

too__ __

__ __ istle

fi __ __

__ __ eese

BRAIN BOX

Digraphs are two letters that make one sound.

Example: **thing**

The **digraph** in this word is **t-h.** When you say **thing,** you don't hear the **t** and **h** sounds separately. You hear the new **th** sound.

Brain Quest Grade 2 Workbook

It Takes Three

Say the word for each picture.

Complete each word with a **consonant cluster** from the boxes.

Blends and consonant clusters

s t r awberry ＿＿＿ ee ＿＿＿ eet

＿＿＿ irrel ＿＿＿ ub ＿＿＿ inkler

＿＿＿ ong ＿＿＿ one ＿＿＿ ay

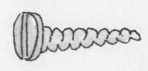

＿＿＿ are ＿＿＿ ew ＿＿＿ ead

Brain Quest Grade 2 Workbook

Lost Letters

Complete each word with a **consonant cluster** from the boxes.

Draw a line from the word to its picture.

st | nk
mp | lt
nd

ba <u>n</u> <u>k</u>

qui __ __

ha __ __

la __ __

toa __ __

BRAIN BOX

A **consonant cluster** is a group of two or three consonants that are next to each other in a word.

Example: land

The **consonant cluster** in this word is **n-d**.

sku __ __

Complete each word with a **consonant cluster** from the boxes.

rd	rk
sk	nt

Draw a line from the word to its picture.

pa <u>r k</u>

te __ __

fo __ __

ma __ __

bi __ __

boa __ __ game

Kite and Circle

Look at the **c** words in the boxes below.

If the word has a **hard c** sound, like **kite**, write the word next to the kite.

If the word has a **soft c** sound, like **circle**, write the word next to the circle.

Hard c and
soft c

come

kite

circle

come	cent
count	care
cellar	card
city	cereal

Goose and Jacket

Look at the **g** words in the boxes below.

If the word has a **hard g** sound, like **goose**, write the word next to the goose.

If the word has a **soft g** sound, like **jacket**, write the word next to the jacket.

Hard g and soft g

giraffe

jacket

giraffe	goat
game	gem
give	giant
genius	grow

goose

BRAIN BOX

The letter g has two sounds: a **hard g** sound as in **girl** and a **soft g** sound as in **giant**.

Picture Cards

Complete each word with a **short vowel**.

short a words

c <u>a</u> t   m __ n

h __ m   __ nt

m __ d   b __ t

short e words

d __ sk   b __ ll

sl __ d   b __ d

h __ n   p __ n

short i words

f __ sh   w __ g

f __ ll   p __ g

l __ d   h __ d

short o words

d __ ll   h __ p

r __ ck   f __ x

n __ t   p __ t

short u words

pl __ m   m __ d

c __ p   b __ s

s __ n   f __ n

Short Vowel Sort

Read the words in the colored boxes.

Write each word next to the picture that has the same **short vowel** sound.

Short vowels

hat	map	big	got	dad
box	red	hug	miss	let
must	pet	mom	up	ran
ten	top	rush	him	fix

short a words

hat

hat

short e words

chest

short i words

milk

short o words

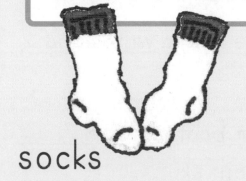

socks

short u words

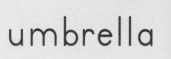

umbrella

At the Bay with Raina

Underline the words that have a long a sound.

Raina is heading to the bay with her family.

Before she leaves, she puts her hair in a braid.

It was raining yesterday, but the sun is shining brightly today.

Write ai or ay to complete the long a words and finish the story.

At the bay, Raina and her brother spr _a y_ on sunblock to protect their skin.

Raina enjoys watching the bay's wildlife, like dolphins and r __ __ s.

The sky has turned gr __ __, and it is time to go home.

Raina decides to p __ __ nt a picture of her special day.

BRAIN BOX

These letter combinations can make a long a sound: ai as in rain, and ay as in ray.

What Do You See?

Write **e**, **ea**, **ee**, or **ey** to complete the **long e** words.

My dad is driving us to the b __ __ ch.

There are thr __ __ of us in the car.

On the way, w __ pass a tr __ __ .

Words with
the long e
sound: e, ea,
ee, ey

There are lots of b __ __ s in the tr __ __ .

They are making hon __ __ .

Luckily, the bees don't sting m __ !

Finally, we reach the s __ __ !

BRAIN BOX

These letter combinations
can make a **long e** sound:
ee as in **wheel**, **ea** as in
flea, and **ey** as in **money**.

Sometimes, the letter e all
by itself can also make a
long e sound, as in **he**.

I Love Riddles!

Write **i**, **ie**, **igh**, or **y** to complete the **long i** words.

Words with the long i sound: i, ie, igh, y

I am not a baby. I am not an adult.
I am a ch _i_ ld.

I help you see in the dark.
I am a flashl __ __ __ t.

Wear me around your neck. I am a t __ __.

I buzz in your ears. I am a fl __.

Long ago, I wore a suit of armor.
I am a kn __ __ __ t.

BRAIN BOX

These letters can make a **long i** sound: y as in **by** and igh as in **high**.

Sometimes these letters can also make a **long i** sound: i as in **find** and ie as in **pie**.

You can't keep a secret from us! We are
sp __ __ s.

You have to peel me.
I am an orange r __ nd.

Let's Roll Along

Write **oa**, **ow**, or **o** to complete the **long o** words.

sailb <u>o</u> <u>a</u> t

t _ _ d

Words with the
long o sound:
oa, ow, o

g _

g _ _ t

c _ ld

r _ _ d

sn _ _

BRAIN BOX

These letter combinations can make a **long o** sound: **oa** as in **float** and **ow** as in **low**.

Sometimes, the letter **o** all by itself can also make a **long o** sound, as in **no**.

26

PHONICS

Words with the
/oo/ sound:
oo, ew, ue, ui

A Few Clues

Write **u**, **ew**, **ue**, or **ui** to
complete the words with
the **oo sound**.

I am the color of the sky.
I am bl <u>u e</u> .

I can be an apple, an orange, or a grape.
I am fr __ __ t.

You can swim in me.
I am a p __ __ l.

The candle was still burning.
The man bl __ __ it out.

I stick things together.
I am gl __ __.

I am a toy that's
still in the box.
I am brand-n __ __.

BRAIN BOX

These letter combinations make
the **/oo/** sound: **ue** as in **due**,
ui as in **juice**, **oo** as in **stool**, and
ew as in **flew**.

Vote for E!

Add an **e** to the end of these **short vowel** words to make new **long vowel** words.

can   can <u>e</u>

man   man __

cap   cap __

cub   cub __

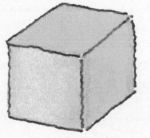

tub   tub __

pin   pin __

BRAIN BOX

A **short vowel** can become a **long vowel** when you add an **e** to the end of some words.

Example:
kit + e = kite

When you add an **e** to the end of **kit**, you get **kite**. Kite has a **long i** sound.

Mix-Ups

Unscramble each word.

Write the correct word on the line.

esiml <u>smile</u>

ateg _____

nbeo _____

becu _____

preo _____

iemd _____

zmea _____

nnei _____

9

Tear and Share

Write **air**, **are**, or **ear** below each picture
to complete the words.

Words with
air, are, ear

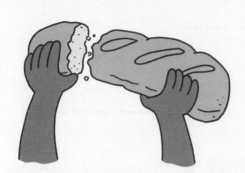

First t e a r,

then sh _ _ _.

They won f _ _ _ _

and squ _ _ _.

Milo had a sp _ _ _,

so he didn't need
a rep _ _ _.

BRAIN BOX

The letter
combinations
are, **ear**, and
air can have
the same
sound.
For example,
care, **wear**,
and **fair**.

Girl with Curls

Write **er**, **ir**, or **ur** to complete the words.

c __ __ tain

g <u>i</u> <u>r</u> l

c __ __ ls

sh __ __ t

f __ __ n

wat __ __

sk __ __ t

BRAIN BOX

The letter combinations **er**, **ir**, and **ur** can all have the same sound. For example, **bird**, **hurt**, and **father**.

Clark's Chores

Write **ar**, **or**, **ore**, or **our** to complete the words.

Cl __ __ k lives on a f __ __ m.

Today, he has ch __ __ __ s to do.

Words with ar, or, ore, our

First, Cl __ __ k feeds the h __ __ se.

He puts hay in the b __ __ n.

He sweeps the p __ __ ch.

He p __ __ __ s milk for the cat.

Then, Cl __ __ k waters the vegetable
g __ __ den.

He makes a list of things he needs from
the st __ __ __ .

BRAIN BOX

When an r follows a vowel, the r slightly changes the vowel sound. Say the words out loud to hear the sounds in words with **ar**, **or**, **ore**, and **our**.

He picks f __ __ __ ears of c __ __ n
for dinner.

Joy and Her Hound Dog

Write **oi**, **oy**, **ou**, or **ow** to complete the word below the pictures.

Then sort the words by sound on the cards.

Diphthongs: oi and oy; ou and ow

cl __ __ n

b __ __

c __ __

m __ __ se

t __ __

c __ __ n

s __ __ l

h __ __ se

oi, oy	**ou, ow**
	clown

The Cook on the Moon

Read the words in the boxes below.

Write the words that have the same vowel sound as **cook** next to the cook.

Write the words that have the same vowel sound as **moon** next to the moon.

Short and long oo sounds

broom	book	food	good
look	noodle	spoon	wood

cook

BRAIN BOX

Sometimes the same letter combinations have different sounds. Two o's together can have a **long oo** sound, as in **moon**, or a **short oo** sound, as in **cook**.

moon

broom

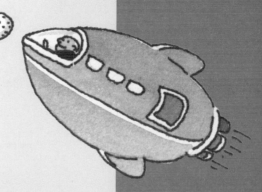

Variant vowel
sounds:
al, all, aw, o

Rhyme Time!

Write **al**, **all**, **aw**, or **o** to complete each rhyme.

b a l l on
the w a l l

w __ __ k and
t __ __ k

m __ th in
the br __ th

str __ __ on
a sees __ __

l __ ng s __ ng

cr __ __ l
and b __ __ l

SPELLING AND VOCABULARY

Shhh—can you find the silent letter in the word g-h-o-s-t? Don't let a hard word like ghost spook you! Studying spelling and vocabulary makes learning new words less of a trick and more of a treat.

PARENTS In this section, children build on the phonics skills they practiced earlier and expand their understanding of how letters combine to form short and long vowel sounds. Children also grow their vocabulary through explorations of antonyms, synonyms, homophones, and plurals.

For additional resources, visit www.BrainQuest.com/grade2

Sort the Shorts

Sort the words below by vowel sound.

Write the words on the correct vowel card.

jet	bath	vest	chick	rod
ink	bus	tag	skunk	sock
rat	spot	neck	luck	mitt

Short vowel review

short a
bath

short e

short i

short o

short u

BRAIN BOX

Look at these **short vowel** words: **hat, bed, rig, rod,** and **cup.** They all have the same spelling pattern:

consonant / short vowel / consonant

You can use this pattern to help you spell similar words.

SPELLING AND VOCABULARY

Short vowel review

Answer the riddles with words from the boxes.

A pen is filled with me. I help you write.
I am i n k.

I am a baby bird. I am a _ _ _ _ _ _ .

I fly high in the sky. I am a _ _ _ .

I am yellow and take you to school.
I am a _ _ _ .

I am black and white and very smelly.
I am a _ _ _ _ _ .

You use me to fish. I am a fishing _ _ _ .

I keep your foot warm and clean.
I am a _ _ _ _ .

You look at me when you want to know the price.
I am a price _ _ _ .

You take me when you get dirty.
I am a _ _ _ _ .

Crossword Craze

Complete the **long vowel** words with a vowel and a **final e**.

Write the words in the puzzle.

Across

2. She _a_ t _e_ the apple.

4. We have a flat t __ r __ .

5. A tree with needles: p __ n __ .

6. Our whole family gets together on New Year's __ v __ .

8. Four plus five equals n __ n __ .

9. A raisin is a dried gr __ p __ .

Down

1. A 3-D map of the world is a gl __ b __ .

3. Those are hers, th __ s __ are mine.

4. Another word for "melody": t __ n __ .

7. Tomatoes grow on a v __ n __ .

9. They g __ v __ the money they collected to charity.

10. Every Sunday I talk to my grandma on the ph __ n __ .

2. a t e

Long a words

Long a Words

Complete each sentence with a **long a** word from the boxes below.

okay   cake   paint

cage   play   mail

Artists like to draw and ___paint___.

The bird is in the _____.

My favorite thing to eat is _____.

The postal worker delivered our _____.

We rehearsed our parts for the _____.

He fell down, but he is _____.

Now sort the long a words on the cards below.

BRAIN BOX

Look for these spelling patterns in **long a** words: **ai** as in **rain**, **ay** as in **ray**, and **a_e** as in **page**.

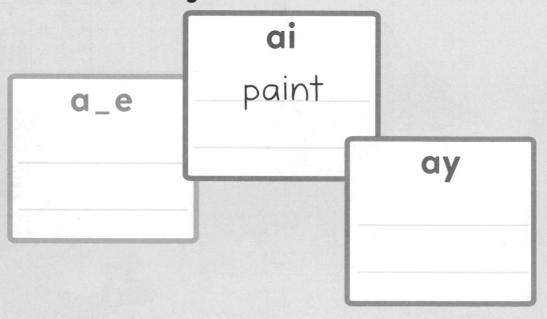

a_e

ai
paint

ay

Long e Words

Complete each sentence with a **long e** word from the boxes below.

sheep	seal	money	dreams
me	Joey	sleep	be

SPELLING AND VOCABULARY

Long e words

My name is _____.

I don't like to _____ tired so I go to bed when it's time to _____.

If I can't fall asleep, I count _____.

I always have sweet _____.

In one dream, I swam like a _____ and found a chest full of _____.

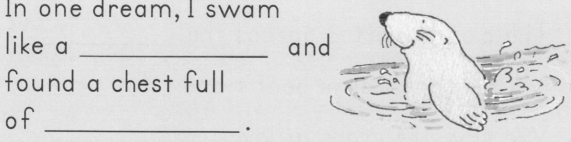

Dreams make _____ happy!

BRAIN BOX

Look for these spelling patterns in **long e** words: **ee** as in **wheel**, **ea** as in **flea**, **ey** as in **money**, and **e** as in **he**.

Now sort the **long e** words on the cards below.

ee

ea

ey

e

Long i Words

Complete each sentence with a **long i** word from the boxes below.

pie	sky	ice	high
bright	tide	rice	twice

Some birds can fly very __high__.

When water freezes, it becomes _____.

The opposite of dark is _____.

In cooking class, she baked an apple ____.

If you checked your work two times, it's done _____.

The clouds drifted across the _____.

My favorite dish is beans and _____.

We saw the crabs at low _____.

BRAIN BOX

Look for these spelling patterns in **long i** words:
y as in **by**,
igh as in **high**,
i as in **find**,
ie as in **pie**, and
i_e as in **kite**.

Now sort the **long i** words on the cards below.

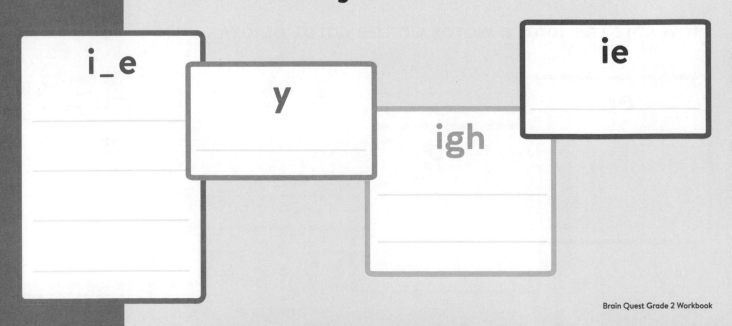

i_e

y

igh

ie

Long o Words

Complete each sentence with a **long o** word from the boxes below.

toast	wrote	rainbow	grow
throat	go	gold	note

At the end of the _____ there is a pot of _____.

I _____ a letter to a friend at camp.

I eat _____ with butter for breakfast.

My mom always puts a _____ in my lunch box.

The opposite of stop is _____.

I'm sick. I have a sore _____.

Every day I _____ bigger.

Now sort the long o words on the cards below.

BRAIN BOX

Look for these spelling patterns in **long o** words: **oa** as in **float**, **ow** as in **low**, **o** as in **no**, and **o_e** as in **rode**.

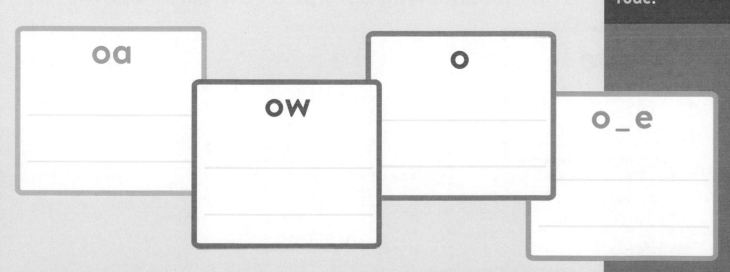

Long u Words

Complete each sentence with a **long u** word from the boxes below.

unicorn	use	utensils	music
argue	huge	mule	cute

A _____ has a horn on its head.

I _____ colored pencils in art class.

When my sister and I disagree,
we _____ .

Puppies and kittens are so _____ !

The opposite of tiny is _____ .

A knife and a fork are eating _____ .

The _____ carried the heavy bags
up the mountain.

I listen to pop _____ .

Now sort the **long u** words on the cards below.

BRAIN BOX

Look for these spelling patterns in **long u** words: ue as in **cue**, u as in **universe**, and u_e as in **cute**.

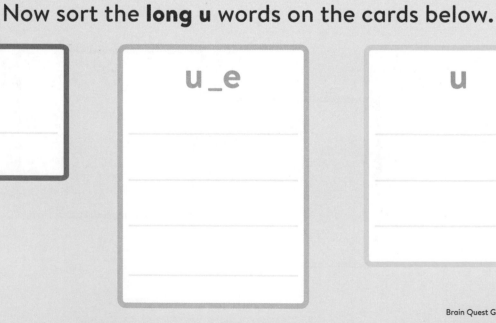

ue	u_e	u

Silent Letters

These words all have **silent letters**.

Say each word out loud as you copy it.

Then circle the silent letter.

comb <u>com(b)</u>

lamb _____

sign _____

knife _____

kneel _____

sword _____

high _____

write _____

sigh _____

Write a sentence using one of the words above.

_____

_____

Words with silent b, g, k, w

BRAIN BOX

A **silent letter** is one that we don't pronounce. Silent letters can appear at the beginning, in the middle, or at the end of words, such as **h**our or **k**noc**k**, dou**b**t or castle, and stoma**ch** or thum**b**.

Compound It!

Use a word from the boxes below to make a compound word.

Use the pictures as clues.

plane	berry	book	robe
fish	pot	hole	cake

pan + _cake_ = _pancake_

air + _____ = _____

bath + _____ = _____

straw + _____ = _____

key + _____ = _____

note + _____ = _____

flower + _____ = _____

gold + _____ = _____

Draw a line from a word in the green column to a word in the blue column to make a common **compound word.**

Then write the compound word in the orange column.

back	cage	backbone
camp	bone	
bag	pole	
book	work	
grape	flakes	
sky	line	
home	pipes	
bean	fire	
bird	case	
snow	vine	

The Why of Y

The words below all end in **y**, but they are not all pronounced the same way.

Sort the words by vowel sound.

Write the **y** words with the same sound as **spy** on the spy card.

Write the **y** words with the same sound as **bunny** on the bunny card.

baby	cry	happy	merry	my
story	fly	mommy	lullaby	sky

spy

_____
_____
_____
_____

bunny

_____
_____
_____
_____
_____

Use words from the boxes above to complete the sentence.

A _____ sings a _____ to her _____ .

A Silly Story

Read the story.

Circle all the words that end in **y**.

Then sort the words on the cards below.

Y words with long e and long i sounds

There once was a gutsy canary. He lived in the city. In January, the tiny bird decided to fly to the country to visit his family. He packed his bag with a supply of food, a library book, and his favorite fuzzy pajamas. Then he flew into the sky. After months of traveling, he finally arrived in July. Everyone was so happy!

"Now it's time to go home," chirped the pretty bird.

"But why?" said his father.

"Because I am shy" was his reply.

y words with long i sound

y words with long e sound

gutsy

Zane's Yard Sale

Complete the words that have the same vowel sound as **yard**.

Words with ar

al <u>a</u> <u>r</u> m clock

j __ __ of m __ __ bles

toy c __ __ s

y __ __ n

toy f __ __ m

shin gu __ __ ds

st __ __ sweater

Spell Like a Shark!

Write all the **ar** words from the boxes below in alphabetical order.

start	party	cart	garden
art	march	park	large
far	hard	harm	bar

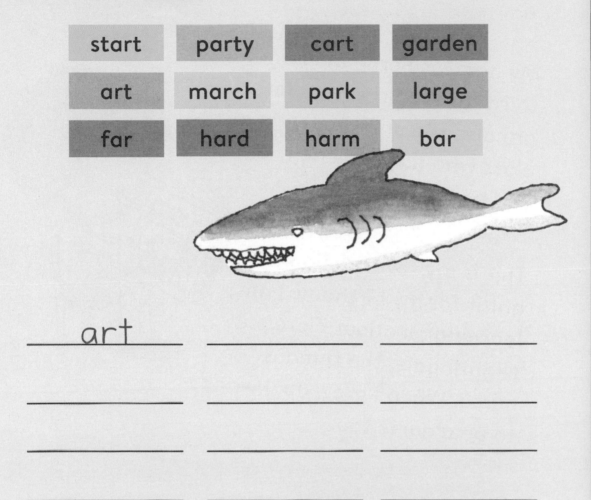

_____art_____   _____   _____

_____   _____   _____

_____   _____   _____

_____   _____   _____

Write two sentences using any of the **ar** words in the above boxes.

_____

_____

_____

_____

All About Fern

Circle all the words that have the same vowel sound as **Fern**.

SPELLING AND VOCABULARY

Words with ear, er, ir, ur

My name is Fern, and I am the third tallest girl in my class. I am also the only person in my class who has curly hair. Can you believe that?

This is my favorite book. I got it for my birthday. I am learning all about Florence Nightingale, the famous nurse. When I grow up, I want to be a nurse too.

Say each word you circled.

Listen to the vowel sound.

Sort the words by spelling pattern on the **ear**, **er**, **ir**, **ur** cards below.

ir

er
Fern

ur

ear

Spell Like a Bird

Say each word in the colored boxes.

Sort the words by spelling pattern on the cards below.

Words with ear, er, ir, ur

pearl	lantern	burn	search
bird	curb	lavender	first
hurt	shirt	letter	earth
purpose	chirp	perfect	glitter
urgent	early	dirty	earn

ur

ear

ir

er

A Cow in the House!

Complete the clues with words that make the *low/* sound.

Write the words in the puzzle.

Words with
ou, ow

Across

1. Milk comes from c<u>o</u> <u>w</u> <u>s</u>.

3. A h__ __ __ __ is a building where you live.

5. Is your hair the color br__ __ __?

7. What goes up must come d__ __ __.

9. A circus cl__ __ __ makes people laugh.

11. I use a t__ __ __ __ to get dry.

Down

2. A tiny animal that likes cheese is a m__ __ __ __.

4. If you lose something, go to the lost and f__ __ __ __.

6. The opposite of "in" is __ __ __.

8. The opposite of "later" is n__ __.

10. To yell something is to sh__ __ __.

12. A king wears a cr__ __ __ on his head.

13. The opposite of "quiet" is l__ __ __.

14. A type of bird that goes hoot is an __ __ __.

Roy Points

Sort the words by spelling pattern on the cards below.

SPELLING AND VOCABULARY

Words with oi, oy

coin	boy	toy
voice	oyster	noise

join	oil	boil	royal	point
loyal	enjoy	choice	annoy	destroy

oi

oy

Moose and Books

All the words in the boxes are **oo** words, but they are not all pronounced the same way.

Write the **oo** words with the same sound as **moose** on the moose card.

Write the **oo** words with the same sound as **book** on the book card.

Words with oo

balloon	hood	spoon	wood	foot
tooth	look	shook	spooky	loose

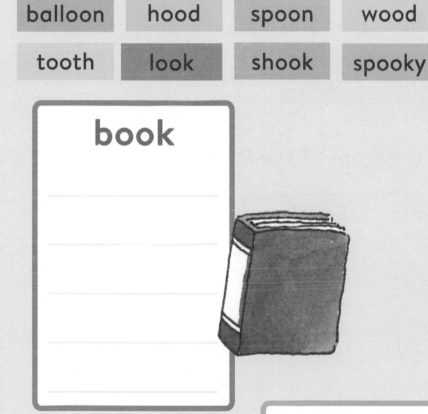

book

_____

_____

_____

_____

_____

moose

_____

_____

_____

_____

_____

Opposites!

Read each sentence.

Circle the **antonym** of the underlined word in the sentence.

A great dane is a <u>large</u> dog!

(small) giant big

The balloon flew <u>up</u> in the air.

high down left

She went to the <u>front</u> of the line.

top start back

It is so <u>hot</u> today!

warm cold rainy

Draw a line from each word to its **antonym**.

terrible   dry

before   thrilled

disappointed   after

soaked   fabulous

BRAIN BOX

Antonyms are words that have opposite meanings. **Happy** and **sad** are antonyms.

So Many Snowflakes!

Synonyms

Draw a line from each snowflake to its **synonym**.

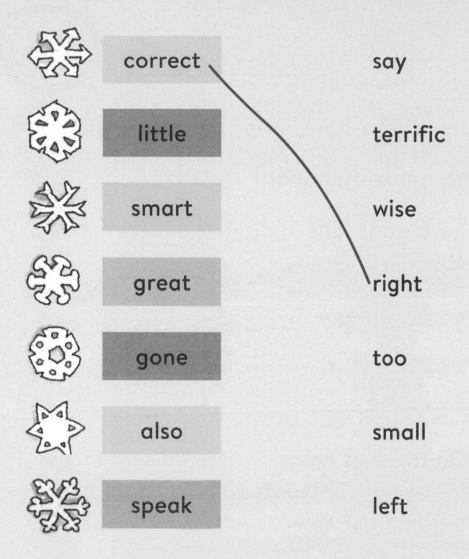

correct — right

little

smart

great

gone

also

speak

say

terrific

wise

right

too

small

left

Fill in the blanks with **synonyms** from the boxes below.

challenging   sparkle   moist   missing

lost _____   difficult _____

shine _____   damp _____

BRAIN BOX

Synonyms are words that have similar meanings. End and finish are synonyms.

Write It Right

Circle the correct **homophone** in each sentence.

Homophones

It is half past the our / hour.

There is a pair / pear tree in the yard.

She broke her right / write leg.

The clouds are hiding the son / sun.

BRAIN BOX

Homophones are words that sound the same but have different spellings and meanings. **Eight** and **ate** are homophones.

On the lines below, write two sentences for two of the words you did not circle.

_____

_____

_____

_____

Same Sounds

Circle the correct **homophone** in each sentence.

I am going to ballet class too / two.

Look at that fish's I / eye!

All the boats are on sale / sail.

The movie is playing for two weaks / weeks only.

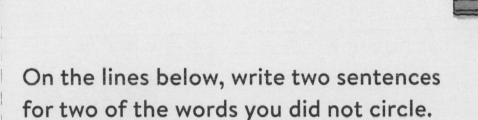

On the lines below, write two sentences for two of the words you did not circle.

_____

_____

_____

_____

More than One

Write the plural for each word by adding **s** or **es**.

SPELLING AND VOCABULARY

Plurals with s, es

apple ___apples___

ax _____

glass _____

box _____

cat _____

sandwich _____

fox _____

pen _____

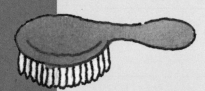

brush _____

crutch _____

BRAIN BOX

Plural means more than one.

Add **s** to make most nouns plural.

Add **es** if the noun ends in **sh, ch, tch, s,** or **x.**

watch _____

bus _____

Irregular Plural

Each box shows a picture of a word that is irregular when plural. Circle the correct irregular plural. Then rewrite the correct answer on the line below it.

Irregular plurals

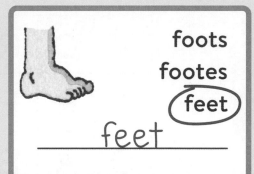

foots
footes
(feet)

feet

wemen
women
womenes

_____

mouse
mice
mouzes

_____

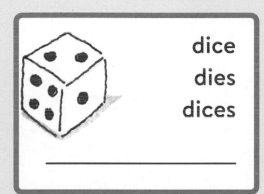

dice
dies
dices

_____

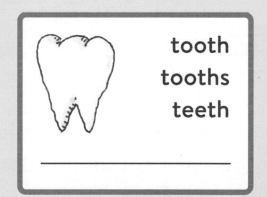

tooth
tooths
teeth

_____

childs
children
childran

_____

BRAIN BOX

Some plurals are **irregular**.

This means you don't add **s** or **es** at the end to make the word plural.

You have to change the whole word.

Color Search

Circle all the color words in the puzzle.

Color words

V	O	R	A	I	G
I	R	E	D	N	R
O	A	B	I	D	E
L	N	L	N	I	E
E	G	U	B	G	N
T	E	E	O	O	W
Y	E	L	L	O	W

Now unscramble the letters you did NOT circle to answer this question:

Where can you find all these colors in nature?

In a _ _ _ _ _ _ _ .

LANGUAGE ARTS

Understanding how to write strong sentences makes us better speakers and writers. We'll learn how to use describing words (adjectives), action words (verbs), and naming words (nouns) to ask questions and share ideas.

PARENTS Building awareness of sentence types and parts of speech improves learners' reading comprehension and helps make your child a more thoughtful writer. Reinforce the learning in this section by pointing out interesting adjectives or verbs in books you read together or by going on a noun hunt and searching for specific objects in and out of the home.

PLACE A STICKER HERE

For additional resources, visit www.BrainQuest.com/grade2

Tell Me About It!

Read each group of words.

Underline the **statements**.

<u>I like to go to the ice cream store.</u>

The pictures on the window.

My mother, my sister, and I.

We eat our favorite flavors.

The chocolate ice cream.

My mom likes vanilla.

The books resting by our feet.

I sit on the bench.

I have red shoes.

BRAIN BOX

A **sentence** is a group of words that express a complete thought.

All sentences begin with a capital letter.

A **statement** is a sentence that explains or tells what someone or something does.

End a statement with a period.

Write each statement correctly.

Begin with a capital letter and end with a period.

the swimming class begins at noon

The swimming class begins at noon.

i can dive off the high board

_____

sara does a backflip

_____

the little kids wear water wings

_____

our lifeguard's name is Rena

_____

Say What?

Rewrite each sentence.

If the sentence asks a **question**, add a question mark.

If the sentence is a **statement**, add a period.

is it raining hard

<u>Is it raining hard?</u>

sam likes his green boots

_____

can we jump in the puddles

_____

will you play with me after school

_____

i hope it stops raining

_____

what did the forecast say

_____

do you see a rainbow

_____

BRAIN BOX

A **question** is a sentence that asks something. End a question with a question mark.

Remember to begin all sentences with a capital letter.

The Race Begins!

Rewrite each sentence as an **exclamation**.

Exclamations
and commands

look how fast I can run

<u>Look how fast I can run!</u>

tie your shoelaces

_____

we love racing

_____

BRAIN BOX

An **exclamation** is a sentence that shows strong feelings, such as surprise, excitement, or fear. End an exclamation with an exclamation point.

A **command** is a sentence that tells someone to do something. End a command with either a period or an exclamation point.

on your mark, get set, go

_____

hurry to the finish line

_____

Oh no! Jamal is still reading when he should be going to sleep.

Write two **commands** that his father might say to him.

_____

_____

A Picture Tells a Story

Write each sentence correctly.

Then circle the type
of sentence it is.

is the skateboard in the closet

Is the skateboard in the closet?

statement   (question)   exclamation   command

wear a hat and a sweater

statement   question   exclamation   command

i think we should go to the park

statement   question   exclamation   command

watch out for the ghost

statement   question   exclamation   command

Sentence Scramble

First, unscramble the words to write a **statement**.

Then use the same words to write a **question**.

Remember to **capitalize** and use correct **punctuation**.

Word order

come   party

they   will

to   the

They will come to the party.

Will they come to the party?

sleep   can

on

bed   dog

my   the

_____

_____

_____

he   get

mail   should

the

_____

_____

cookie   can

jar   I   open

the

_____

_____

Cookies

Flor R.
212 Oak Street
New York, NY 11111

Jane Smith
42 Maple Street
Townville, Kansas 55555

Common
nouns

People, Places, and Things

Underline the **nouns** in each sentence.

The <u>students</u> borrowed <u>books</u> from the <u>library</u>.

The baker sold bread at the market.

The teacher brought his guitar to school.

The children sat on the grass in the park.

The president of the country made a speech.

The captain sailed her ship down the river.

The farmer grew corn on their farm.

My sister is the top speller in our state.

The waiter wears a uniform to the restaurant.

The pilot landed the plane at the airport.

Now sort all the **nouns** you underlined on the cards.

people

students

places

library

things

books

Common nouns

BRAIN BOX

A **noun** is a part of speech that names a person, place, thing, or idea. **Parent, city, computer, and happiness** are all nouns.

And Away We Go!

Underline the **proper nouns** in each sentence.

Proper nouns

Dina walked across the Golden Gate Bridge in San Francisco.

In New York, Ramon went to the top of the Empire State Building.

Mrs. Li taught us that the Nile River flows through Cairo.

BRAIN BOX

A **proper noun** is a word that names a specific person, place, or thing. Proper nouns are always capitalized.

William went to Paris to see the painting of the Mona Lisa.

Now fill in the box with the **proper nouns** you just underlined.

people

places

things

Write a postcard to a friend about somewhere you have visited.

Circle all the **proper nouns.**

Dear _____ ,

_____

_____

_____

name

address

Sincerely,

_____

Proper nouns

Things I Like!

Fill in the notes with your favorites.

Remember to capitalize each proper noun.

More proper nouns

My favorite holiday is:

My favorite day of the week is:

My birthday is:

BRAIN BOX

The names of holidays, months, and days of the week are all **proper nouns.**

The titles of books, movies, TV shows, magazines, and newspapers are also proper nouns.

Remember to capitalize proper nouns.

My favorite book is:

My favorite movie is:

My favorite TV show is:

Fun at the Playground!

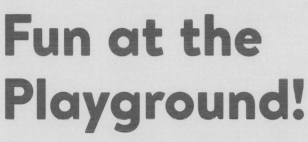

The words in the circles are all **pronouns.**

Pronouns

She   We   It   He   They

Rewrite each sentence using the pronoun that can take the place of the underlined word(s) in each sentence.

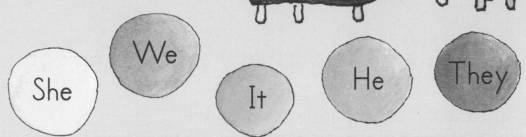

Max and Lila are on the seesaw.

They are on the seesaw.

Juan swings through the air.

_____

Amy zooms down the slide.

_____

All of us are having a good time.

_____

The playground is busy.

_____

BRAIN BOX

A pronoun is a word that can take the place of a noun.

Dog Day

Underline the **subject** of each sentence.

Circle the **noun**.

The <u>park</u> is a busy place.

Ollie walks his dogs there every afternoon.

The biggest dog is named Hamlet.

Ollie's favorite is a poodle named Fifi.

The pets run and play together.

Some dogs bark at the squirrels.

The squirrels stay in the trees.

BRAIN BOX

The **subject** tells who or what a sentence is about.

The subject always has a **noun** or a **pronoun** in it.

Batter Up!

Choose a word from a baseball to complete each sentence.

 swings

The batter _picks_ up the bat.

 holds

She _____ up to home plate.

 hits

The catcher _____ up her mitt.

 steps

The pitcher _____ the ball.

 picks

The batter _____.

 throws

She _____ the ball.

Write a sentence describing your favorite sport.

Underline the **verb** in your sentence.

_____

_____

_____

Brain Quest Grade 2 Workbook

BRAIN BOX

A **verb** is an action word. It tells what someone or something does.

Bake a Cake!

Underline the **verb** in each sentence.

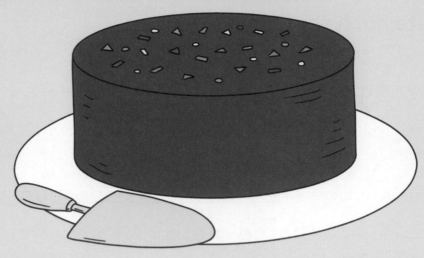

Malik mixes the cake batter in a bowl.

Carla pours the batter into a pan.

Dad puts the pan in the oven.

Ding! Dad takes the cake out of the oven.

Write two sentences about what Carla and Malik will do next.

Underline the **verbs** in your sentences.

_____

_____

_____

_____

Visit the Farm!

Change the underlined **verb** so that
the action happened in the past.

LANGUAGE ARTS

Malik and Carla <u>visit</u> a local farm.

Yesterday, Malik and Carla <u>visited</u>
a local farm.

Present- and
past-tense verbs

Carla <u>likes</u> to feed the chickens.

Carla _____ to feed the chickens.

Malik <u>looks</u> for the goat.

Malik _____ for the goat.

Carla <u>opens</u> the door to the barn.

Carla _____ the door to the barn.

Malik <u>walks</u> the horse inside.

Malik _____ the horse inside.

Carla and Malik <u>enjoy</u>
their time at the farm.

Carla and Malik _____
their time at the farm.

Time to Paint

These sentences are written in present tense, then past tense. Fill in the blanks with the past- or present-tense form of **to have**.

Irregular verbs: to have

I **have** paints.   I __had__ paints.

He **has** brushes.   He _____ brushes.

We _____ fun.   We **had** fun.

They **have** canvases.   They ____ canvases.

Now use the correct form of the verb **to have** to answer these questions.

What color eyes do you have?

I _____.

BRAIN BOX

The verb **to have** is irregular. This means it doesn't follow the same rules as most regular verbs.

to have

present tense		past tense
(I have)	=	(I had)
(You have)	=	(You had)
(He / She / It has)	=	(He / She / It had)
(We / They have)	=	(We / They had)

What favorite toy did you have as a baby?

I _____

_____.

Time for a Picnic!

Fill in the correct form of the verb **to be** to complete each sentence.

Circle *present* if the verb tells about the **present**.

Circle *past* if the verb tells about the **past**.

Irregular verbs:
to be

The picnic __was__ last Sunday.

present   (past)

Today it _____ raining.

present   past

Luckily, the weather _____ dry last week.

present   past

We _____ in the park until it got dark.

present   past

I _____ tired when I got home from the picnic.

present   past

I _____ glad to be inside now.

present   past

BRAIN BOX

The verb **to be** is irregular. This means it doesn't follow the same rules as most regular verbs.

to be

present tense		past tense
I am	=	I was
You are	=	You were
He / She / It is	=	He / She / It was
We / They are	=	We / They were

To Have and to Be

Use a form of **to have** or **to be** to answer each question.

What is the weather like today?

_____

What was the weather like yesterday?

Irregular
verbs: to be,
to have

_____

Do you have an umbrella today?

_____

Draw a picture of you and a friend in the picture frame.

Then answer the questions below.

I _____ _____ years old.

My best friend _____ _____ years old.

This year, we _____ in the _____ grade.

Last year, we _____ in the _____ grade.

Who Did What?

Use the drawings to help you match the **subjects** to the **predicates**.

Draw a line from the words in the SUBJECT column to the matching words in the PREDICATE column.

Subjects and predicates

SUBJECT	PREDICATE
The family	painted the sign.
Lia	squeezed each lemon.
Ken	sold the lemonade.
Their parents	cut the lemons in half.

Write sentences using the subjects and predicates you matched. Circle the noun(s) in the **subject**. Underline the verb in the **predicate**.

The (family) sold the lemonade.

_____

_____

_____

BRAIN BOX

The naming part of a sentence is called the **subject**. It tells who or what the sentence is about.

The telling part of a sentence is called the **predicate**. It tells what the subject does.

Day at the Carnival

Look at each picture and read the caption.

Circle the **noun**.

Underline the **adjective**.

white horse

two prizes

red apples

tall clown

tiny lamb

three flags

BRAIN BOX

A **noun** names a person, place, or thing.

An **adjective** tells about or describes a noun.

Color, size, and number words are adjectives.

Write the **adjectives** under the correct headings on the chart.

Then add two more adjectives to each list.

Adjectives

color words	number words	size words
white	two	tiny

Write three sentences using the new adjectives you added.

_____

_____

_____

_____

Five Senses

Circle the **noun** in each caption.

Underline the **adjective.**

salty popcorn

loud noise

stinky cheese

wet elephant

colorful balloons

delicious hot dog

Write **look, feel, taste, smell,** or **sound** by the correct body parts below.

smell

BRAIN BOX

Adjectives can tell
how nouns look, feel,
taste, smell, or sound.

Where? When? How?

The **verb** in each sentence has been underlined.
Circle the **adverb**.

LANGUAGE ARTS

(Yesterday) we <u>found</u> the treasure map.

Adverbs

It <u>was hidden</u> upstairs.

We <u>screamed</u> loudly when we found it.

BRAIN BOX

Adverbs tell where, when, or how something happens.

An **adverb** can tell more about a **verb**.

Now we <u>will hunt</u> for treasure.

The treasure <u>is buried</u> under the tree.

Example: Tomorrow, we will eat ice cream.

Tomorrow is the adverb because it tells when we will eat ice cream.

<u>Can</u> we <u>find</u> it quickly?

Write each **adverb** you circled on the correct card below.

Where?	When?	How?
	yesterday	

Bear Bakes

Underline the **verb** in each sentence.

Circle the **adverb**.

Bear <u>went</u> (inside) to bake apples.

He washed the apples carefully.

Afterward, he put them in the oven.

Later, he saw they were done.

He took the tray from the oven slowly.

He will sell the apples outside at the market.

Write each **adverb** you circled on the correct card below.

Where?

inside

When?

How?

READING

Do you know how to become a stronger reader? By READING a lot! What is your favorite book or story? Write it here:

_____

PARENTS Myths, fables, plays, news, short stories—there are so many different genres to read! Help your child develop a love of reading by spending time reading together each day. Research shows the best way to become a good reader is to read, read, and read some more.

PLACE A STICKER HERE

A Poem

Read this poem told from a child's point of view.

Bed in Summer

Robert Louis Stevenson

In winter I get up at night
And dress by yellow candlelight.
In summer, quite the other way,
I have to go to bed by day.

I have to go to bed and see
The birds still hopping on the tree,
Or hear the grown-up people's feet
Still going past me in the street.

And does it not seem hard to you,
When all the sky is clear and blue,
And I should like so much to play,
To have to go to bed by day?

"Bed in Summer" is a poem that rhymes.

Fill in the chart with **rhyming words** that end the lines of the poem. Then add your own rhyming word.

night	way	see

feet	you	play

Now answer the questions.

How does the child in the poem feel?

_____

_____

How do you feel in the summertime?

_____

_____

A Fable

Read the story.

Answer the questions for each part of the story.

Fable

The Wind and the Sun

An Aesop Fable

One bright, sunny day, Wind blew in. The trees bowed down. The windows in a farmhouse shook.

Wind boasted, "I am Wind and I am strong! I am stronger than trees. I am stronger than windows. I am stronger than Sun!"

Sun came out from behind a cloud. Sun said, "Wind, you are strong. But I am stronger than you."

"No!" said Wind. "I am stronger than you!"

Sun said, "Let us have a contest to see who is stronger."

1

"Yes!" said Wind. "We will have a contest!" Sun looked down and saw an old man strolling by. He wore a hat and an overcoat. "Do you see that old man?" Sun asked. "Whichever of us can make him take off his overcoat is the strongest. Wind, I will let you go first." Then Sun hid behind a cloud to watch.

Wind huffed. Wind puffed. Wind began to blow. The trees bowed down even lower. The windows in the farmhouse shook louder. Wind blew strong and cold.

The man said, "Brrr! What a cold, strong wind!" Then he buttoned up his overcoat. Wind blew stronger. Wind blew colder.

(continued on next page)

2

Who are the main characters in the story?

_____

_____

With each gust of cold air, the old man stayed huddled inside his overcoat.

Sun came out from behind the cloud. "Now it is my turn." Sun smiled. Bright rays of sunlight filled the air. The air grew warmer.

The old man said, "Ah! The sun feels nice and warm." Then he unbuttoned his overcoat.

Sun shone brighter and brighter. The old man felt warmer and warmer. He said, "The sun is very strong. I feel very warm. I do not need my overcoat." And the old man took off his overcoat.

Sun said, "I win."

"You win this time," Wind said. "Next time, *I* will pick the contest!"

THE END

3

What challenge do Sun and Wind agree to?

_____

_____

What happened when Wind blew?

_____

_____

What happened when Sun shone?

_____

_____

Who won the contest?

_____

_____

What would happen if Rain came along and
entered the contest?

_____

_____

How does having a contest solve an argument?

_____

_____

What's Cooking?

Read the recipes.

Make up a name for each recipe. Write it on the line.

Recipe

_____
recipe name

INGREDIENTS:
· banana
· blueberries
· grapes
· strawberries

DIRECTIONS:
1. Slice the banana into round pieces.
2. Wash the blueberries, grapes, and strawberries.
3. Slice the strawberries in half.
4. Mix the fruit in a bowl.

_____
recipe name

INGREDIENTS:
· banana
· slice of bread
· peanut butter

DIRECTIONS:
1. Slice the banana into round pieces.
2. Toast a slice of bread.
3. Spread peanut butter on the toast.
4. Put the banana slices on top of the peanut butter.

_____
recipe name

INGREDIENTS:
· banana
· $\frac{1}{2}$ cup vanilla yogurt
· $\frac{1}{2}$ cup granola

DIRECTIONS:
1. Cut the banana into small pieces.
2. Put the yogurt in a bowl.
3. Sprinkle the fruit and granola on top.

What dish can you make?

Draw a picture of the dish.

List the ingredients.

Write the steps in order.

Give your dish a name.

Recipe

_____
recipe name

INGREDIENTS:

- _____

- _____

- _____

- _____

DIRECTIONS:

1. _____

2. _____

3. _____

4. _____

Yum!

A Myth

Read the story.

Answer the questions for each part of the story.

How Day and Night Came to Be
An Inuit Myth

When the world was very young, there was only darkness. Ice covered the land. Two children, a boy and a girl, lived in a small cabin. They hunted for food. It was hard work. It was tiring work. There was no time to play.

One day, a stranger came to their door. He was part man, part raven. He asked the children to come out and play. The children were too tired to play. They offered the Raven Man food and drink.

"No, thank you," said the Raven Man.

1

Why was there no time for the children to play?

_____

_____

"But if you can solve this puzzle, I will reward you." He gave them a small bag and left.

In the bag were many small fish bones. By the pale light of a small lamp, the children arranged the bones into the shape of the fish. They solved the Raven Man's puzzle.

Their reward was a fishing spear. The sharp barbs on the spear made hunting easier. Then the Raven Man gave the children a second puzzle of bones. The children put the pieces together to make the flipper of a seal. Again, the Raven Man rewarded them.

The Raven Man's second gift was an oil lamp large enough for cooking and heating. With each gift, the Raven Man made life a little easier for the children. Then the Raven Man took out a ball. He said, "Now let's play."

(continued on next page)

2

Outside in the freezing darkness, the children and the Raven Man played catch. Suddenly the ball caught on the Raven Man's sharp beak. The ball ripped open. Through the tear, the sun escaped and lit the sky. For the first time, the world felt the warmth of sunshine.

And that is how day was created out of night.

THE END

3

What was inside the ball the children were playing with?

_____

_____

What two gifts did the Raven Man give
the children?

_____

_____

How do you think the children feel at the end of the
story? Why?

_____

_____

How would this story ending be different if the visitor
were a Rabbit Man instead of the Raven Man?

_____

_____

What happened first, next, and last?

Number the pictures to show the order.

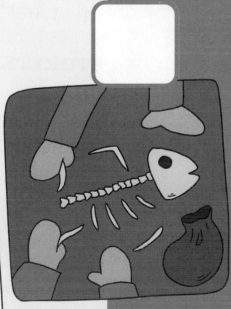

A Play

Read the play out loud, by yourself, or with friends. Then answer the questions at the end of the play.

Buying the Shade
A Folktale from Japan

STORYTELLER: Once there lived a mean, rich old man. One afternoon, the mean old man took a nap under a tree near his house. When he woke up, he saw a young man also enjoying the shade.

OLD MAN: Go away, young man! This is my shade!

YOUNG MAN: Sir? Why is this your shade? I thought this tree belonged to the village.

OLD MAN: Ha! My great-great-grandfather planted this tree! This tree and its shade belong only to me!

STORYTELLER: The young man thought, "I shall teach the old man a lesson."

YOUNG MAN: Then, sir, I wish to buy the shade from your tree.

STORYTELLER: The old man thought, "I shall take the young man's gold!"

1

OLD MAN: You may buy my shade for five pieces of gold!

YOUNG MAN: Done!

STORYTELLER: Now the old man was quite pleased with himself. He was five pieces of gold richer. He put the gold in his pocket and went back to his big house.

Later that afternoon, the sun began to set. The shadow of the tree grew and grew, until it covered the old man's house. The young man walked into the old man's house.

OLD MAN: What are you doing in my house? Get out of here!

YOUNG MAN: The shade of the tree covers this house. The shade belongs to me. Now the house belongs to me too.

STORYTELLER: In anger, the old man left the village forever. The clever young man moved into the big house.

YOUNG MAN (to the whole village): People, please come and enjoy the shade of the tree!

STORYTELLER: And they did.

THE END

2

Plot the play you just read.

Tell what happens in the **beginning**, **middle**, and **end** of the play.

Beginning Why won't the old man let the young man rest under the tree?

_____

_____

_____

Middle What does the young man do next?

_____

_____

_____

End How does the story end?

_____

_____

_____

Can you think of a different ending for the folktale? Write it here.

_____

_____

_____

A Short Story

Read the story.

Cause and effect

Monday Morning

One Monday morning, Lena turned off the radio and put an umbrella in her backpack. The backpack was so stuffed, the umbrella stuck out.

On her way to school, Lena saw her friends Grace and Justin. "Hey, Lena," called Grace. "Wait up."

Grace and Justin caught up with Lena.

"What's that sticking out of your backpack?" asked Grace.

"My umbrella," said Lena. "What's that sticking out of your backpack?"

"My soccer shin guards," Grace said. "We have practice today."

"I don't think so," said Lena.

"We always have soccer practice on Mondays," said Justin.

"Not when it rains," Lena said.

(continued on next page)

1

BRAIN BOX

A **cause** tells why something happens.

An **effect** is what happens.

The three children looked up at the sun in the bright blue sky.

"It won't rain today," said Grace.

"I listened to the radio this morning," Lena said.

"And what did the weather report say?" Justin asked. "Did it say there will be no soccer practice this afternoon?"

Lena laughed. "Well, almost! The forecast is for thunderstorms this afternoon."

THE END

2

Draw a line to match each **cause** and **effect**.

Causes

| Effects
---|---

Lena learned it was going to rain.

They put their shin guards in their backpacks.

Grace and Justin play soccer on Monday.

They talk and joke together.

Lena, Grace, and Justin are friends.

She took an umbrella to school.

Write three other titles for this story.

Circle the one you like best.

_____

_____

_____

Goddesses

Read these myths about goddesses.
Myths are narrative tales that are
usually about supernatural beings.

Characters

In ancient Greek mythology, there was a contest to give the best gift to a new city. **Athena**, the goddess of wisdom, battled against Poseidon, the god of the sea. Poseidon hit the ground with his spear. This drew water out of the ground. The fountain of water was beautiful. But the water was salty, and the people could not drink it. Athena, in her wisdom, planted an olive tree, which gave the people food to eat. Athena won, and that city—Athens, Greece—was named after her.

Freya was the Morse goddess of love and beauty. She drove a chariot pulled by two cats. She wore a gold necklace that she never took off. Loki, the god of mischief, wanted the necklace for himself. One night, Loki—who could change himself into different forms—turned himself into a fly. While Freya slept, Loki snuck into her room and stole the necklace. Then he raced to the sea, where he turned into a seal and swam away. But the watchman of the gods had been by the shore. He also turned himself into a seal and went after Loki. The two "seals" fought. The watchman won and returned the necklace to Freya.

Who is who? Write the name of the character in the picture on the line below it.

_____

_____

_____

_____

A Folktale

Read the story. Then answer the questions.

Anansi and the Talking Melon

A Folktale from Africa

Long, long ago in Africa, there lived a spider named Anansi. He was clever but also very lazy. Anansi made his home in a thorn tree that overlooked Elephant's melon patch. Every day, Elephant weeded and watered the melons. Every day, the melons grew bigger and riper. Every day, Anansi's appetite for melons grew bigger too.

One hot summer afternoon, Elephant weeded and watered his melon patch. Then he left the garden. Anansi really wanted one of Elephant's melons!

What do you think Anansi will do next?

I predict that Anansi will

Anansi took a thorn from his thorn tree and lowered himself into Elephant's garden. Clever Anansi picked the best melon. He used the thorn to make a hole in it. Then the hungry spider crawled inside.

Anansi ate. He ate and ate and ate, until he could eat no more. Finally, Anansi tried to crawl out of the hole. But he was stuck! He had eaten too much, and now the hole was too small. How would Anansi get out?

What is Anansi's problem?

_____

_____

_____

What caused Anansi's problem?

_____

_____

_____

The clever spider thought up a clever plan. As Elephant walked by the melon, Anansi said loudly and clearly, "I am the king!"

"Who said that?" asked Elephant.

"I did," said Anansi from inside the melon. "I am the king!"

(continued on next page)

Surprised, Elephant said, "You're a melon, not a king! But a talking melon is rare. I will take you to the king."

Elephant presented the melon to the king. The king said, "Why have you brought me a melon, Elephant? I have melons of my own."

"Not like this one, Your Majesty," said Elephant.

Then the melon said, "I am the king!"

"Who said that?" demanded the king angrily.

How does the king feel? Why does he feel that way?

_____

_____

_____

"I did," said the melon. "I am the king!"

"You are not the king! You are a melon!" roared the king. Then the king took the melon and threw it.

The melon sailed through the air all the way back to Elephant's garden. The melon landed SPLAT! and cracked wide open. Anansi jumped out and scurried up a coconut tree.

Elephant returned home. He said to his melons, "You are melons. Just melons! Not kings!"

From behind a coconut, Anansi said, "Melon kings! How silly!"

Elephant looked up into his coconut tree and cried, "Oh no! Talking coconuts!"

THE END

How did Anansi solve his problem?

_____

_____

_____

Imagine That!

Write your own poem, fable, myth, short story, folktale, or play on the page below.

Don't forget to write the title on the first line.

WRITING

Have you ever wanted to interview an alien? What about write your own recipe? You'll get to try both in this next section!

PARENTS This section includes a variety of writing exercises to inspire your child's creativity. Don't worry about spelling and grammar—the ideas are more important than writing mechanics. Sharing the writing you do regularly, like text messages and grocery lists, provides a model of everyday writing.

PLACE A STICKER HERE

For additional resources, visit www.BrainQuest.com/grade2

Alien Interview

Write a **question** for each human to ask the alien about life on another planet.

WRITING

Asking questions

Who _____

_____ ?

What _____

_____ ?

Where _____

_____ ?

Why _____

_____ ?

When _____

_____ ?

How _____

_____ ?

Write an **answer** from the alien for each question.

_____
_____.

_____
_____.

_____
_____.

_____
_____.

_____
_____.

_____
_____.

Diary entry

What a Day!

Imagine you were one of the kids who met the alien from another planet.

Write about what you and your new alien friend did.

Dear Diary,

_____

_____

_____

_____

_____

_____

_____ ,

_____
your name

What Is a Wocnix?

Wocnix is a made-up word.

What do you think it is? A flower? An animal?

You decide. Draw a picture of a wocnix in the box.

> **Wocnix**

Write sentences to describe the wocnix.

What does it look like? _____

_____

What does it sound like? _____

_____

What does it feel like? _____

_____

How does it taste? _____

How does it smell? _____

Fill Me In!

Read the story and fill in the missing words.

Give your story a title.

Title: _____

Today is _____, the first day
day of the week

of _____ vacation. I put on my
season

favorite _____ . _____
clothing   family member

and I made _____ for
food

_____ .
meal

It tasted _____ ! Then we went to
how something tastes

_____ . The first thing we did
fun place

was _____ . After that, we
activity #1

_____ . By the time we got
activity #2

home, it was _____ .
time of day

What a _____ day!
adjective

Draw a picture to illustrate your story.

Word categories

Step by Step

Read the recipe. Then answer the questions.

Super Sundae

INGREDIENTS:

- banana
- vanilla ice cream
- chocolate ice cream
- strawberry ice cream
- chocolate sauce
- whipped cream

DIRECTIONS:

1. Slice the banana lengthwise.

2. Put the banana in the bowl.

3. Add 1 scoop of vanilla, 1 scoop of chocolate, and 1 scoop of strawberry ice cream.

4. Cover with chocolate sauce.

5. Add whipped cream.

What is the first step?

_____

What is the last step?

_____

How do you make your favorite food?

Write the recipe below.

_____

recipe name

INGREDIENTS:

- _____
- _____
- _____
- _____
- _____
- _____

Writing directions

DIRECTIONS:

1. _____

2. _____

3. _____

4. _____

5. _____

6. _____

Be a Reviewer

Choose a book you like. Follow the steps below to write a book review.

Book title: _____

Author: _____

What is the book about?

_____

_____

What did you like about the book?
Give a reason for your opinion.

_____

_____

What didn't you like?
Give a reason for your opinion.

_____

_____

What happened in your favorite part of the book?

_____

_____

BRAIN BOX

A review tells what the reader or viewer thinks about book, movie, or other work.

Now think of a movie you like and write a
movie review.

Movie title: _____

Starring: _____

What is the movie about?

_____

_____

What did you like about the movie?
Give a reason for your opinion.

_____

_____

What didn't you like?
Give a reason for your opinion.

_____

_____

What happened in your favorite part of the movie?

_____

_____

_____

Story starters

And Then . . .

Read the beginning of each story.

Write about what happens next.

Then draw a picture.

I woke up early because my back itched. I got out of bed and looked in the mirror. I couldn't believe my eyes! I had wings!

_____

_____

_____

_____

Story starters

The balloon seller handed me a brown balloon. He winked and said, "Be careful. This one is magic!"

_____

_____

_____

_____

Story starters

My friends and I played hide-and-seek in the park. I hid behind a big oak tree. I saw a small sign on the trunk. It said: PLEASE KNOCK TWO TIMES. So I did.

_____

_____

_____

_____

CURSIVE

Did you know people started writing cursive letters to be able to write faster? Give it a try, starting one letter at a time. At the end of the section, you'll be well on your way to being a (speedy) cursive expert!

PARENTS Because of our increased use of technology, we use much less cursive than we did in the past. It's helpful for students, though, because cursive uses different brain skills than print—writing both ways is like your brain doing exercises to stay healthy. Remind your child that mistakes are expected when learning a new skill and their effort is what's important.

PLACE A STICKER HERE

A Is for Alexis

**Trace the letters.
Then write them.**

a a a

a a a

a a a

Trace the sentence.

Alexis asks

Amanda

about Alaska.

B Is for Ben

Trace the letters.
Then write them.

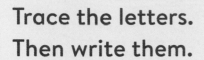

B B B

b b b

b b b

Trace the sentence.

Ben buys

brownies

from Blake.

C Is for Carmen

**Trace the letters.
Then write them.**

C C C

C C C

C C C

Trace the sentences.

Carmen can

canoe. Can

you?

D Is for David

Trace the letters.
Then write them.

D, d

D D D

d d d

d d d

Trace the sentence.

David dives

down into the

deep sea.

E Is for Eric

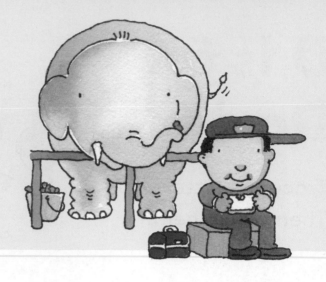

Trace the letters.
Then write them.

E E E

e e e

e e e

Trace the sentence.

Eric eats with

Edna the

elephant.

F Is for Francesca

Trace the letters.
Then write them.

F F F

f f f

f f f

Trace the sentence.

Francesca

finally fixes

the fence.

G Is for Garret

**Trace the letters.
Then write them.**

G G G

g g g

g g g

Trace the sentence.

Garret got a guitar from Grandma.

H Is for Hannah

Trace the letters.
Then write them.

H H H

H, h

h h h h

h h h

Trace the sentence.

Hannah has a

horse named

Harry.

I Is for Ina

**Trace the letters.
Then write them.**

l l l

i i i

i i i

Trace the sentence.

Ina ice-skates

around an

igloo.

J Is for Juan

Trace the letters.
Then write them.

$\mathcal{J}$ $\mathcal{J}$ $\mathcal{J}$

j j j

j j j

Trace the sentence.

Juan just put the jellyfish in the jar.

K, k

K Is for Kayla

**Trace the letters.
Then write them.**

$\mathcal{K}$ $\mathcal{K}$ $\mathcal{K}$

k k k

k k k

Trace the sentence.

Kayla keeps

her kitten in

the kitchen.

L Is for Lauren

Trace the letters.
Then write them.

ℒ ℒ ℒ

ℓ ℓ ℓ

ℓ ℓ ℓ

Trace the sentence.

Lauren loves

lemons and

limes.

M Is for Manuel

**Trace the letters.
Then write them.**

m m m

m m m

m m m

Trace the sentence.

Manuel

makes a

monster mask.

N Is for Nicole

Trace the letters.
Then write them.

n n n

n n n

n n n

Trace the sentence.

Nicole needs

one more

nickel.

O Is for Omar

**Trace the letters.
Then write them.**

O, o

𝒪 𝒪 𝒪

𝑜 𝑜 𝑜

𝑜 𝑜 𝑜

Trace the sentence.

Omar owns

a goat named

Olive.

P Is for Pia

Trace the letters.
Then write them.

CURSIVE

P, p

P P P

p p p

p p p

Trace the sentence.

Pia paints

a pig named

Petunia.

Q Is for Quinn

**Trace the letters.
Then write them.**

2 2 2

q q q

q q q

Trace the sentence.

Quinn eats

a quarter of

the quiche.

R Is for Rajeev

Trace the letters.
Then write them.

R R R

r r r

r r r

Trace the sentence.

Rajeev reads

about rowdy

rabbits.

S Is for Shantel

Trace the letters.
Then write them.

S S S

s s s

s s s

Trace the sentence.

Shantel

stretches before

sprinting.

T Is for Trung

**Trace the letters.
Then write them.**

T, t

1 2 *T T T*

2 1 *t t t*

t t t

Trace the sentence.

Trung sets up

his tent under

the tree.

U Is for Uma

**Trace the letters.
Then write them.**

U U U

u u u

u u u

Trace the sentence.

Uma lives

upstairs from

Ursula.

152

CURSIVE

U, u

Brain Quest Grade 2 Workbook

V Is for Victor

**Trace the letters.
Then write them.**

V, v

$\mathcal{V} \quad \mathcal{V} \quad \mathcal{V}$

$v \quad v \quad v$

$v \quad v \quad v$

Trace the sentence.

$\mathcal{V}ictor \; visits$

$\mathcal{V}elma \; and$

$\mathcal{V}ance.$

Brain Quest Grade 2 Workbook

W Is for Will

CURSIVE

W, w

**Trace the letters.
Then write them.**

U U U

w w w

w w w

Trace the sentence.

Will wears a

wild wig on

Wednesdays!

X Is for Xena

Trace the letters.
Then write them.

x x x

x x x

x x x

Trace the sentence.

Xena has an

extra special

X-ray.

CURSIVE

Y, y

Y Is for Yolanda

**Trace the letters.
Then write them.**

$\mathcal{Y}$ $\mathcal{Y}$ $\mathcal{Y}$

y y y

y y y

Trace the sentence.

Yolanda eats

yummy

yogurt.

Z Is for Zack

Trace the letters.
Then write them.

Z, z

Z Z Z

Z Z Z

Z Z Z

Trace the sentence.

Zack feeds a

zebra at the

zoo.

My Favorite Things

Use your best handwriting to name your favorite:

Book:

Movie:

TV show:

Food:

Sport:

Color:

MATH SKILLS

Can you write numbers as words and words as numbers? Do you know how to skip count and to identify numbers by place value? Let's practice these important math skills!

thousands	hundreds	tens	ones
2	3	4	2

2,342

Place a STICKER here

Bundles of Bugs

Look at the **numerals** and words on each jar.

Write the number they equal on the line.

Place value
to tens

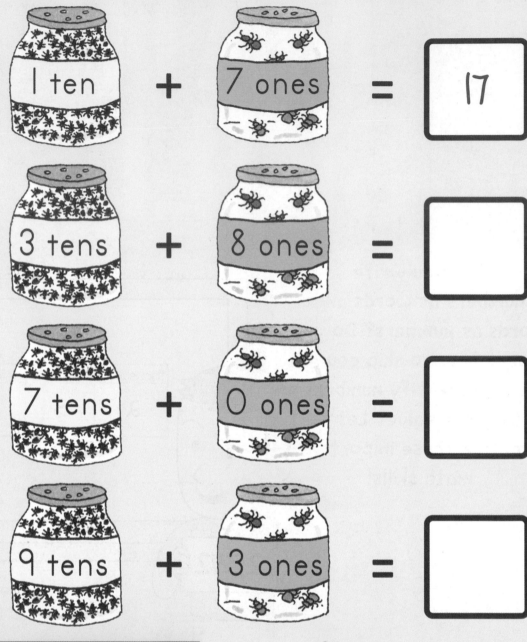

1 ten + 7 ones = **17**

3 tens + 8 ones =

7 tens + 0 ones =

9 tens + 3 ones =

BRAIN BOX

Place value tells us the value of each digit
in a number. Look at **36**:

tens	ones
3	**6**

The **3** tells us there are **3** tens.
The **6** tells us there are **6** ones.

Hop to It!

Circle the correct **numeral**.

Circle the ones.   1 2 ③

Circle the tens.   4 5

Circle the hundreds.   8 3 6

Circle the tens.   5 1 7

Circle the hundreds.   3 8 2

Circle the ones.   6 9 7

Place value
to hundreds

	hundreds	tens	ones
624	6	2	4
391	___	___	___
105	___	___	___
879	___	___	___
243	___	___	___

BRAIN BOX

A 3-digit number is made up of hundreds, tens, and ones. Look at **834**:

hundreds	tens	ones
8	**3**	**4**

The **8** tells us there are **8** hundreds. The **3** tells us there are **3** tens. The **4** tells us there are **4** ones.

Lucky Thousands

Write the **place value** for each numeral on the chart.

Place value to thousands

	thousands	hundreds	tens	ones
1,843	1	8	4	3
2,692	___	___	___	___
7,034	___	___	___	___
4,880	___	___	___	___
9,718	___	___	___	___

Draw a line to match the words to the number.

8 thousands, 5 hundreds, 3 tens, 5 ones   **9,101**

9 thousands, 1 hundred, 0 tens, 1 one   **6,464**

6 thousands, 4 hundreds, 4 tens, 6 ones   **6,446**

6 thousands, 4 hundreds, 6 tens, 4 ones   **8,535**

BRAIN BOX

A 4-digit number is made up of thousands, hundreds, tens, and ones.
Look at **4,627**:

thousands	hundreds	tens	ones
4	**6**	**2**	**7**

The **4** tells us there are **4** thousands. The **6** tells us there are **6** hundreds.
The **2** tells us there are **2** tens. The **7** tells us there are **7** ones.

Words to Numbers

Draw a line to match the number to the words.

 21   1 ten, 2 ones

 1,586   3 hundreds, 1 ten

 310   1 thousand, 5 hundreds, 8 tens, 6 ones

301   2 tens, 1 one

 1,856   3 hundreds, 1 one

 12   1 thousand, 8 hundreds, 5 tens, 6 ones

Write the value of each digit in **452** using words:

_____

_____

Words to Numbers

Write the numbers on the apples.

Write the numerals

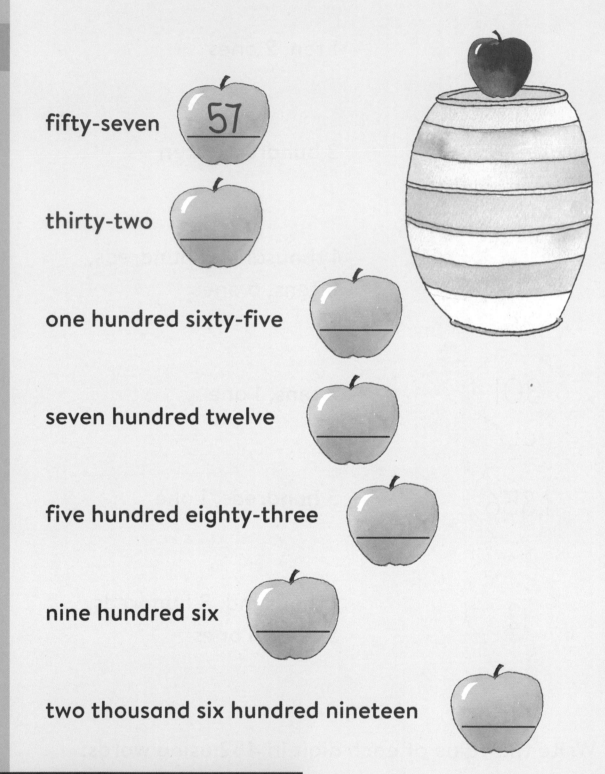

fifty-seven   57

thirty-two   _____

one hundred sixty-five   _____

seven hundred twelve   _____

five hundred eighty-three   _____

nine hundred six   _____

two thousand six hundred nineteen   _____

BRAIN BOX

Numbers can be written with words or numerals.

52 in word form is fifty-two.

1,014 in word form is one thousand fourteen.

My Numbers

Write how many of each you have in the chart below.

Parents	Siblings	Pets	Grand-parents	Aunts	Uncles

Personal numbers

Which do you have the most of? _____

Least? _____

Are any the same number? _____

Complete the sentences with numbers.

Then write each number in word form.

I am _____ years old. _____

I am _____ inches tall. _____

I weigh _____ pounds. _____

You're Invited!

Numbers on fancy invitations are written in word form.

Finish this fancy invitation to your next birthday party. Spell out all the numbers.

Birthday Party!

_____
your name

is turning _____ *years old on*
your age

_____ _____ ,
month   day

_____ .
year

You're invited to a party on the

_____ *of* _____
day   month

at _____
street address

_____ , _____ .
city   state

Compare the Candles

Write the number of candles beneath each cake.

Then write > or < to show which cake has more.

 12   <   13

Greater than, less than

_____   _____

_____   _____

_____   _____

BRAIN BOX

< means **less than.**

> means **greater than.**

Example: 4 < 6

The **less than** sign tells us that **4** is less than **6**

Example: 10 > 5

The **greater than** sign tells us that **10** is greater than **5.**

Counting Crabs

Count the number of crabs sitting on each rock.

Then write > or < to show which rock in each pair has more crabs.

Greater than, less than

$\underline{10} \quad < \quad \underline{13}$

_____ _____ _____

_____ _____ _____

_____ _____ _____

Count by Twos!

Start at 2. Write the missing numbers on the pearl necklace.

Count by twos

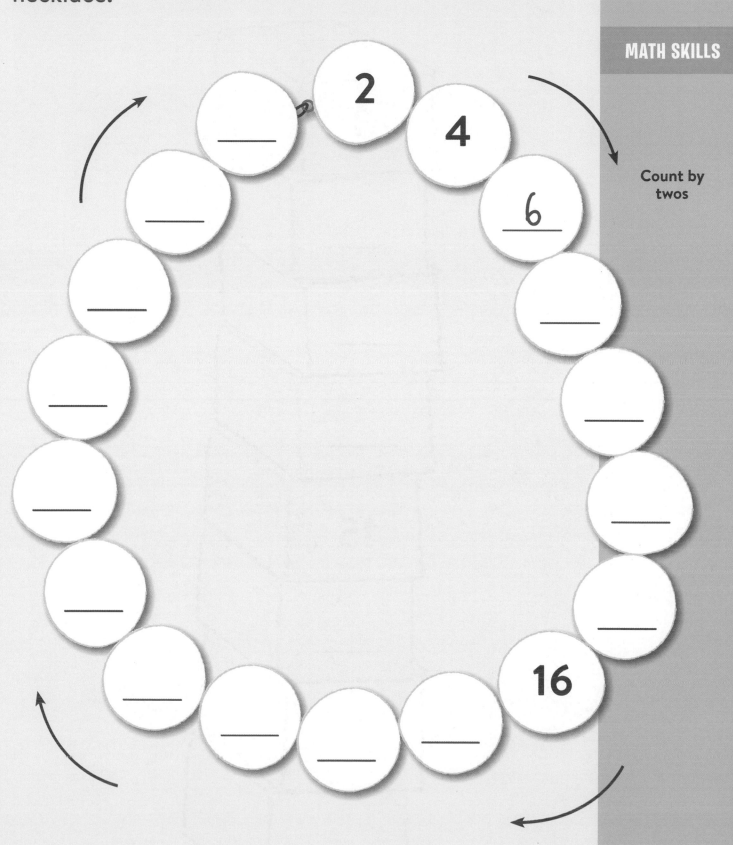

Count by Threes!

Write the missing numbers on the blocks.

Count by threes

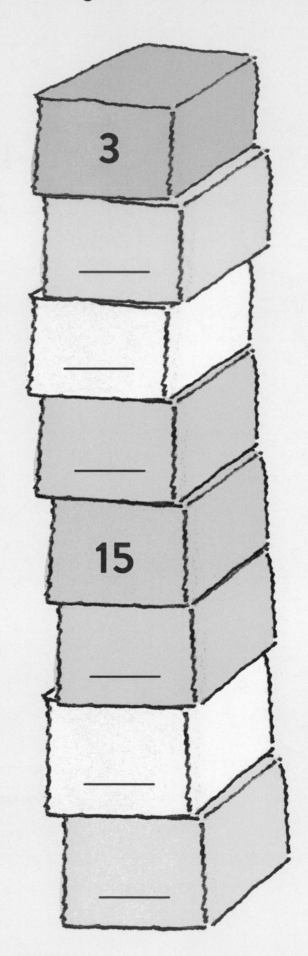

3

_____

_____

_____

15

_____

_____

_____

Count by Fours!

Start at 4. Write the missing numbers on the cars.

Count by fours

If there were 4 more cars on the Ferris wheel, what number would be on the last car?

Count by Fives!

Write the missing numbers on the flags.

5

Count by fives

___ ___ 20 ___ ___ ___

40 ___ ___ 55 ___ ___ ___

75 ___ ___ ___ ___ 100

If the third row had 6 more flags, what number would be last?

___

Count by Tens!

Write the missing numbers on the shirts.

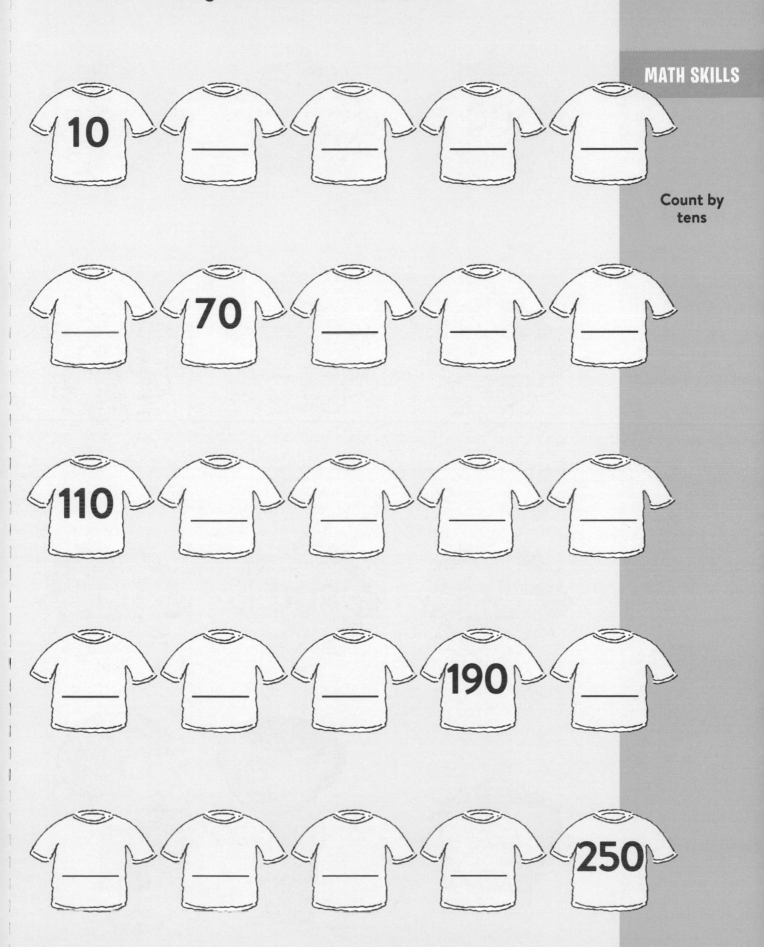

Count by tens

10 ___ ___ ___ ___

___ 70 ___ ___ ___

110 ___ ___ ___ ___

___ ___ ___ 190 ___

___ ___ ___ ___ 250

Count by Hundreds!

Write the missing numbers on the suns.

Count by hundreds

 100

 _____

 _____

 _____

 _____

 600

 _____

800

_____

ADDITION AND SUBTRACTION

You're probably pretty good at addition and subtraction already, so let's make this more challenging by adding and subtracting with three-digit numbers!

PARENTS Learners extend their understanding of addition and subtraction by solving increasingly complex problems. They begin with single-digit numbers and apply the same operations and concepts to greater numbers as the section progresses.

PLACE A STICKER HERE

For additional resources, visit www.BrainQuest.com/grade2

Addition in the Sky

Add the numbers in each balloon.

If all the sums do not equal the number on the basket, cross out the balloon.

Adding
single-digit
numbers

6 + 2 = _____

4 + 4 = _____

2 + 6 = _____

2 + 7 = _____

1 + 3 = _____

2 + 2 = _____

4 + 0 = _____

3 + 1 = _____

8

4 + 3 = _____

2 + 5 = _____

5 + 2 = _____

3 + 4 = _____

7

Adding
single-digit
numbers

8 + 7 = _____

6 + 9 = _____

7 + 8 = _____

5 + 9 = _____

15

5 + 5 = _____

7 + 3 = _____

8 + 2 = _____

2 + 8 = _____

10

3 + 9 = _____

9 + 3 = _____

7 + 5 = _____

8 + 4 = _____

12

3 + 3 = _____

4 + 1 = _____

1 + 4 = _____

2 + 4 = _____

6

Go Fish!

Finish the **fact families**. Write the missing numbers.

Fact families

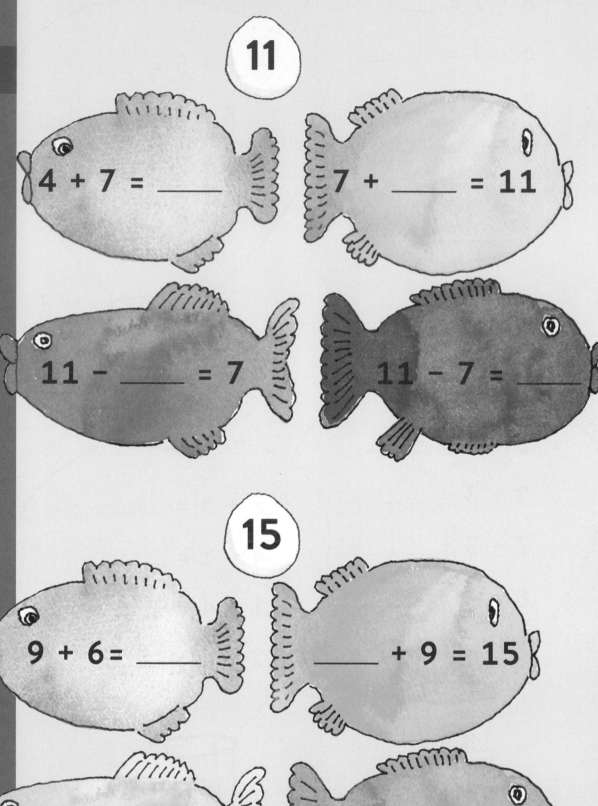

11

4 + 7 = _____

7 + _____ = 11

11 - _____ = 7

11 - 7 = _____

15

9 + 6 = _____

_____ + 9 = 15

15 - _____ = 6

15 - 6 = _____

ADDITION AND SUBTRACTION

Fact families

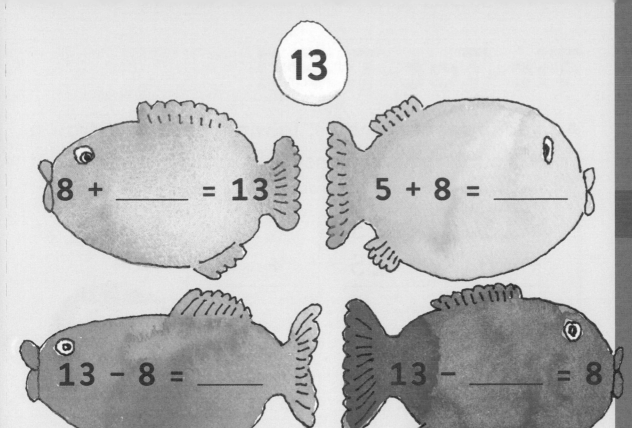

13

8 + _____ = 13

5 + 8 = _____

13 – 8 = _____

13 – _____ = 8

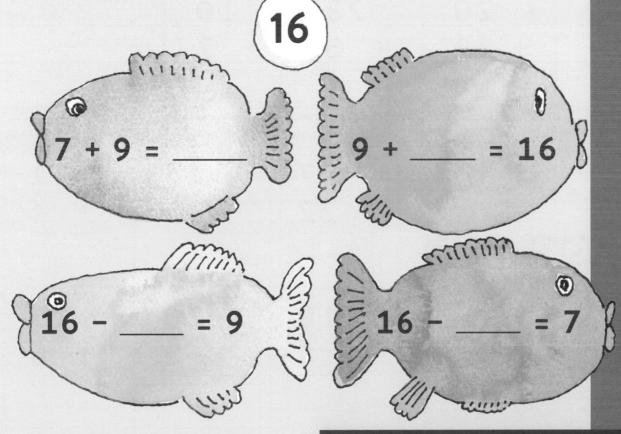

16

7 + 9 = _____

9 + _____ = 16

16 – _____ = 9

16 – _____ = 7

BRAIN BOX

Addition facts can help you solve subtraction problems.

It helps to think about equations as families:

6+2=8	8–2=6
2+6=8	8–6=2

Tic-Tac-Total

Add each set of numbers. To win tic-tac-toe, draw a line through the three answers that are the same.

Adding double-digit numbers

11 + 6	23 + 15	14 + 4
17 + 22	14 + 3	21 + 16
20 + 39	23 + 5	10 + 7

BRAIN BOX

Example:
$$\begin{array}{r} 22 \\ + 15 \\ \hline \end{array}$$

Step 1: Add the numbers in the ones column.
$$\begin{array}{r} 2\,2 \\ + 1\,5 \\ \hline 7 \end{array}$$

Step 2: Add the numbers in the tens column.
$$\begin{array}{r} 2\,2 \\ + 1\,5 \\ \hline 3\,7 \end{array}$$

The answer is **37**.

27 + 22	14 + 5	21 + 4
10 + 8	20 + 5	13 + 6
22 + 3	10 + 7	28 + 31

On the Bus

Time for school!

The school bus made six stops on the way to school.

This chart shows how many students boarded at each stop:

Bus Stop 1:	12 students
Bus Stop 2:	7 students
Bus Stop 3:	9 students
Bus Stop 4:	17 students
Bus Stop 5:	11 students
Bus Stop 6:	8 students

Adding double-digit numbers

How many students boarded at stops 3 and 5 altogether?

_____

How many students boarded at stops 1 and 4 altogether?

_____

How many students boarded at stops 2 and 6 altogether?

_____

Bonus! How many students boarded the bus in all?

_____

Tic-SubTract-Toe

Subtract the numbers. To win tic-tac-toe, draw a line through the three answers that are the same.

Subtracting double-digit numbers

19 – 5	25 – 4	38 – 26
15 – 2	26 – 13	28 – 15
27 – 5	28 – 11	30 – 10

BRAIN BOX

Example: 2 6
– 1 2

Step 1: Subtract the numbers in the ones column.

2 | 6
– 1 | 2
   | 4

Step 2: Subtract the numbers in the tens column.

2 | 6
– 1 | 2
1 | 4

The answer is **14**.

21 – 10	28 – 2	18 – 4
29 – 11	15 – 4	31 – 21
25 – 20	27 – 1	23 – 12

Camping Trip!

Subtract to solve the problems.

There were 48 campers on the trip. 22 campers brought a compass. How many campers did NOT bring a compass?

$$48 - 22 = 26$$

Subtracting double-digit numbers

The campsite has 32 picnic tables. The campers only use 12. How many picnic tables are the campers NOT using?

Marta brought 16 oranges. She gave some to other campers and had 5 left. How many oranges did she give away?

In the lake, Max swims 11 laps. Ari swims 3 fewer laps than Max. How many laps did Ari swim?

On a hike, Leo and Kim spot 27 butterflies. Six of them are white, and the rest are yellow. How many butterflies are yellow?

Colorful Math

Add or **subtract.**

Then use the key to color the spaces.

Addition and
subtraction

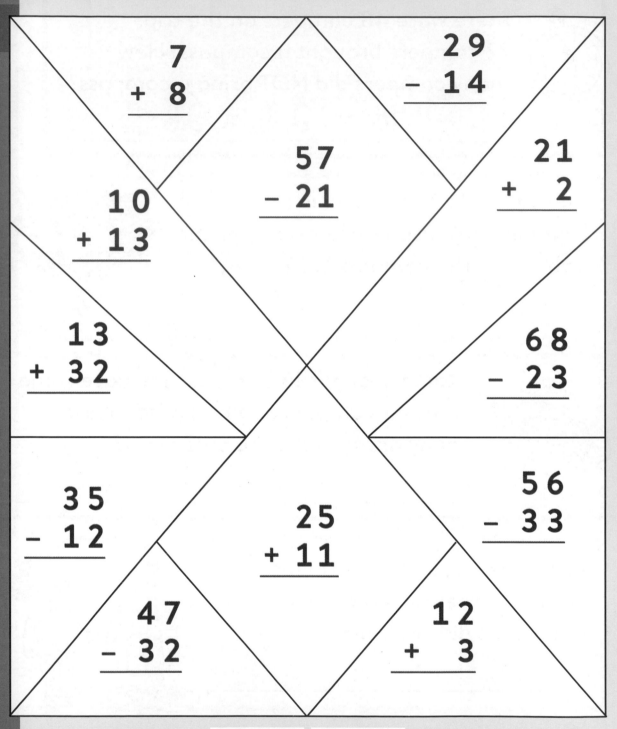

Answer	Color
15	Red
23	Blue
36	Yellow
45	Green

$$12 + 10$$

$$89 - 16$$

$$99 - 53$$

$$99 - 64$$

$$46 + 12$$

$$89 - 31$$

$$13 + 22$$

$$26 + 20$$

$$31 + 42$$

$$57 - 35$$

Answer	Color
22	Pink
73	Purple
35	Gray
46	Orange
58	Brown

Break the Code

Add or subtract.

Adding and subtracting three-digit numbers

```
  112
+  35
-----
  147
```
A

```
  359
- 123
-----
```
C

```
  242
+ 114
-----
```
D

```
  987
- 556
-----
```
E

```
  439
- 125
-----
```
H

```
  171
+ 114
-----
```
I

```
  223
+ 344
-----
```
O

```
  587
- 114
-----
```
V

BRAIN BOX

Example:
```
  321
+ 123
-----
```
The answer is **444**.

Step 1: Add the numbers in the ones column.

```
3 | 2 | 1
+1 | 2 | 3
---------
   |   | 4
```

Step 2: Add the numbers in the tens column.

```
3 | 2 | 1
+1 | 2 | 3
---------
   | 4 | 4
```

Step 3: Add the numbers in the hundreds column.

```
3 | 2 | 1
+1 | 2 | 3
---------
4 | 4 | 4
```

Use your answers to decode the riddle.

Adding and subtracting three-digit numbers

Riddle:

What did the sick spy say to the healthy spy?

Answer:

$$\underline{\quad} \quad \underline{\quad} \quad \underset{285}{\underline{\quad}} \quad \overset{A}{\underline{\quad}} \quad \underline{\quad} \quad \underline{\quad} \quad \overset{A}{\underline{\quad}} \quad \underline{\quad} \quad \underline{\quad} \quad \underline{\quad} \quad \underline{\quad}$$

285   314 147 473 431   147   236 567 356 431

BRAIN BOX

Example:	Step 1: Subtract the numbers in the ones column.	Step 2: Subtract the numbers in the tens column.	Step 3: Subtract the numbers in the hundreds column.
3 4 5 − 1 2 3	3 4 5 − 1 2 3 ___ 2	3 4 5 − 1 2 3 _ 2 2	3 4 5 − 1 2 3 2 2 2
The answer is **222**.			

Math Riddle

Add or subtract.

Adding and subtracting three-digit numbers

```
  263
+ 135
─────
   C
```

```
  244
+ 125
─────
   E
```

```
  889
- 531
─────
  358
   U
```

```
  893
- 451
─────
   G
```

```
  222
+ 345
─────
   H
```

```
  764
- 651
─────
   I
```

```
  312
+ 173
─────
   L
```

```
  687
- 351
─────
   N
```

```
  775
- 450
─────
   Y
```

```
  241
+ 151
─────
   R
```

```
  551
+ 132
─────
   T
```

```
  453
+ 226
─────
   O
```

```
  778
- 524
─────
   S
```

Use your answers to decode the riddle.

Adding and subtracting three-digit numbers

Riddle:

How can you tell if an elephant is under your bed?

Answer:

$$\overline{325}\ \overline{679}\ \overline{358}\ \overline{392}\qquad \overline{336}\ \overline{679}\ \overline{254}\ \overline{369}$$

$$\overline{683}\ \overline{679}\ \overline{358}\ \overline{398}\ \overline{567}\ \overline{369}\ \overline{254}\qquad \overline{683}\ \overline{567}\ \overline{369}$$

$$\overline{398}\ \overline{369}\ \overline{113}\ \overline{485}\ \overline{113}\ \overline{336}\ \overline{442}$$

Math Pun

Add using regrouping.

Addition with regrouping

$$
\begin{array}{r}
{}^{1}38 \\
+\ 8 \\
\hline
46
\end{array}
$$

A

$$
\begin{array}{r}
15 \\
+38 \\
\hline
\end{array}
$$

S

$$
\begin{array}{r}
54 \\
+18 \\
\hline
\end{array}
$$

T

$$
\begin{array}{r}
31 \\
+19 \\
\hline
\end{array}
$$

I

$$
\begin{array}{r}
26 \\
+\ 9 \\
\hline
\end{array}
$$

B

$$
\begin{array}{r}
25 \\
+16 \\
\hline
\end{array}
$$

N

$$
\begin{array}{r}
58 \\
+26 \\
\hline
\end{array}
$$

K

BRAIN BOX

Sometimes you need to regroup numbers when you add. **Regrouping** means to rearrange a number according to its place value to make it easier to work with.

Look at the example below. Just like with other addition problems, add the digits in the ones column first. The sum is 14, which can be represented by 14 ones or by 1 ten and 4 ones. You can't put 14 in the ones column, so you have to regroup.

Example:

$$
\begin{array}{r}
28 \\
+36 \\
\hline
\end{array}
$$

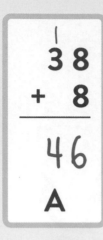

Tens Ones

28 is 2 tens and 8 ones

36 is 3 tens and 6 ones

6 tens + 4 ones

Step 1. Write the 4 below the ones column and write the 1 (which represents one group of 10) above the tens column.

$$
\begin{array}{r}
{}^{1}\ \ \\
2\ |\ 8\ | \\
+3\ |\ 6\ | \\
\hline
|\ 4
\end{array}
$$

Step 2. Then add the digits in the tens column, including the one you wrote on top.

$$
\begin{array}{r}
{}^{1}\ \ \\
2\ |\ 8 \\
+3\ |\ 6 \\
\hline
6\ |\ 4
\end{array}
$$

The answer is **64.**

```
  23
+ 69
─────
  L
```

```
  68
+ 19
─────
  O
```

```
  77
+ 17
─────
  R
```

```
  38
+ 29
─────
  G
```

Use your answers to decode the riddle.

Riddle:

Where do dogs park their cars?

Answer:

__	__		__	A	__	__	__	__	__
50	41		35	46	94	84	50	41	67

__	__	__	__
92	87	72	53

Subtraction Action

Subtract using regrouping.

ADDITION AND SUBTRACTION

Subtraction with regrouping

$$
\begin{array}{r}
^{5\ \ 13} \\
\not{6}\not{3} \\
-\ 17 \\
\hline
46
\end{array}
$$

$$
\begin{array}{r}
55 \\
-\ 28 \\
\hline
\end{array}
$$

$$
\begin{array}{r}
74 \\
-\ 59 \\
\hline
\end{array}
$$

$$
\begin{array}{r}
92 \\
-\ 58 \\
\hline
\end{array}
$$

BRAIN BOX

Sometimes you need to **regroup** numbers to subtract.

Step 1: Like with other subtraction, start with the ones column. You can regroup by taking one group of 10 from the tens column and turning it into 10 ones. 32 is three groups of 10 and 2 ones. Cross out the 3 and write 2 above it to show that there are now two groups of 10. Add the 10 ones to the 2 in the ones column to make 12 ones. Cross out the 2 and write 12 above it.

$$
\begin{array}{r}
^{2\ \ 12} \\
\not{3}\ \ \not{2} \\
-\ 1\ \ 8
\end{array}
$$

Step 2. Now you can subtract 8 from 12 in the ones column, which equals 4.

$$
\begin{array}{r}
^{2\ \ 12} \\
\not{3}\ \ \not{2} \\
-\ 1\ \ 8 \\
\hline
4
\end{array}
$$

Example:

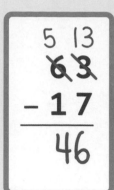

Tens Ones

$$
\begin{array}{r}
32 \\
-\ 18
\end{array}
$$

32 is 3 tens and 2 ones

18 is 1 ten and 8 ones

− = 1 ten   − = 4 ones

Step 3. Now you can subtract 1 from 2 in the tens column, which equals 1.

$$
\begin{array}{r}
^{2\ \ 12} \\
\not{3}\ \ \not{2} \\
-\ 1\ \ 8 \\
\hline
1\ \ 4
\end{array}
$$

The answer is **14**.

$$\begin{array}{r} 97 \\ -49 \\ \hline \end{array}$$

$$\begin{array}{r} 25 \\ -6 \\ \hline \end{array}$$

$$\begin{array}{r} 74 \\ -38 \\ \hline \end{array}$$

$$\begin{array}{r} 83 \\ -27 \\ \hline \end{array}$$

90 – 32 = _____

76 – 18 = _____

Subtraction with regrouping

$$\begin{array}{r} 92 \\ -34 \\ \hline \end{array}$$

$$\begin{array}{r} 28 \\ -19 \\ \hline \end{array}$$

$$\begin{array}{r} 87 \\ -19 \\ \hline \end{array}$$

$$\begin{array}{r} 22 \\ -13 \\ \hline \end{array}$$

82 – 59 = _____

70 – 12 = _____

$$\begin{array}{r} 73 \\ -15 \\ \hline \end{array}$$

$$\begin{array}{r} 43 \\ -34 \\ \hline \end{array}$$

$$\begin{array}{r} 58 \\ -29 \\ \hline \end{array}$$

$$\begin{array}{r} 33 \\ -29 \\ \hline \end{array}$$

Hundreds of Gumballs

ADDITION AND SUBTRACTION

Add using regrouping.

Adding three-digit numbers with regrouping

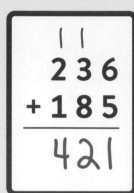

```
  1 1
  2 3 6
+ 1 8 5
-------
  4 2 1
```

```
  2 1 7
+ 2 1 7
-------
```

```
  2 6 5
+ 1 9 8
-------
```

How many blue gumballs?

How many red gumballs?

How many purple gumballs?

How many green gumballs?

$$\begin{array}{r} 209 \\ +212 \\ \hline \end{array}$$

How many yellow gumballs?

$$\begin{array}{r} 162 \\ +199 \\ \hline \end{array}$$

How many pink gumballs?

$$\begin{array}{r} 177 \\ +206 \\ \hline \end{array}$$

BRAIN BOX

Sometimes you need to **regroup** when adding three-digit numbers.

First add the ones column. If the sum is more than 9, **regroup**. Move the 1 to the tens column.

$$\begin{array}{r} 1 \\ 246 \\ +179 \\ \hline 5 \end{array}$$

Next, add the tens column. If the sum is more than 9, **regroup**. Move the 1 to the hundreds column.

$$\begin{array}{r} 11 \\ 246 \\ +179 \\ \hline 25 \end{array}$$

Now add the hundreds column.

$$\begin{array}{r} 11 \\ 246 \\ +179 \\ \hline 425 \end{array}$$

The answer is **425**.

Example:

$$\begin{array}{r} 246 \\ +179 \\ \hline \end{array}$$

246 is 2 hundreds, 4 tens, and 6 ones

179 is 1 hundred, 7 tens, and 9 ones

4 hundreds + 2 tens + 5 ones

Snowflake Subtraction

Subtract using **regrouping**.

Subtracting three-digit numbers with regrouping

$$\begin{array}{r} 862 \\ -489 \\ \hline \end{array}$$

$$\begin{array}{r} 6\ 11\ 11 \\ \cancel{721} \\ -694 \\ \hline 27 \end{array}$$

$$\begin{array}{r} 655 \\ -566 \\ \hline \end{array}$$

$$\begin{array}{r} 333 \\ -244 \\ \hline \end{array}$$

$$\begin{array}{r} 257 \\ -199 \\ \hline \end{array}$$

$$\begin{array}{r} 415 \\ -339 \\ \hline \end{array}$$

$$\begin{array}{r} 332 \\ -142 \\ \hline \end{array}$$

197

ADDITION AND
SUBTRACTION

Subtracting
three-digit
numbers with
regrouping

$$587 - 198$$

$$543 - 268$$

$$770 - 306$$

BRAIN BOX

Sometimes you need to **regroup** when subtracting three-digit numbers.

First subtract the numbers in the ones column. Can you subtract 8 ones from 5 ones? No.
Regroup by taking 1 ten from the tens column and turning it into 10 ones in the ones column.
1 ten and 5 ones equal 15 ones.

Subtract 8 from 15.

$$\begin{array}{r} {\scriptstyle 2\ 15} \\ 3\ \not{3}\ \not{5} \\ -1\ 9\ 8 \\ \hline 7 \end{array}$$

Example:

	Hundreds	Tens	Ones
335			
−198			

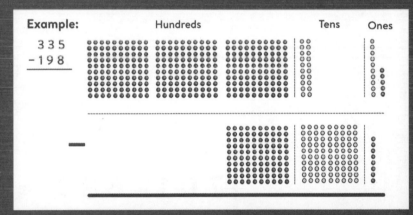

Next subtract the numbers in the tens column. Can you subtract 9 tens from 3 tens? No.
Regroup by taking 1 hundred from the hundreds column and turning it into 10 tens in the
tens column. 10 tens and 2 tens equal 12 tens.

Subtract 9 tens
from 12 tens

$$\begin{array}{r} {\scriptstyle 2\ 12\ 15} \\ \not{3}\ \not{3}\ \not{5} \\ -1\ 9\ 8 \\ \hline 3\ 7 \end{array}$$

Example:

	Hundreds	Tens	Ones

Then subtract the hundreds.
Can you subtract 1 hundred
from 2 hundreds?
Yes.

The answer is **137**.

$$\begin{array}{r} {\scriptstyle 2\ 12\ 15} \\ \not{3}\ \not{3}\ \not{5} \\ -1\ 9\ 8 \\ \hline 1\ 3\ 7 \end{array}$$

Math Concentration

Add or subtract using regrouping.

Color the two cards with matching answers.

$236 + 145$

$673 - 328$

$943 - 136$

$100 - 88 = \underline{\hspace{1cm}}$

$476 - 387 = \underline{\hspace{1cm}}$

$701 - 689 = \underline{\hspace{1cm}}$

$847 - 374$

$311 + 729$

$669 - 288$

MULTIPLICATION AND FRACTIONS

A fraction is a whole split into equal parts. Knowing fractions is helpful when you want to share a pizza, a sandwich, or a chocolate bar. Are you hungry to practice fractions yet?

PARENTS Here's where all that skip counting pays off! Multiplying is repeated addition: 3 x 5 is three groups of five, or skip counting by five three times: 5, 10, 15. Fractions are another form of equal groups. Help your child find real-life examples of fractions next time you eat pizza or cut a tray of brownies!

PLACE A STICKER HERE

For additional resources, visit www.BrainQuest.com/grade2

Times Fly

Finish the **addition** and **multiplication** sentences for each picture.

Addition and multiplication

$2 + 2 + \underline{2} + \underline{2} = \underline{8}$

$4 \times 2 = \underline{8}$

$3 + \underline{} + \underline{} + \underline{} + \underline{} = \underline{}$

$\underline{} \times 3 = \underline{}$

BRAIN BOX

Multiplication is repeated addition—just quicker!

Example: Here are **3** cards. Each card has **4** birds.

How many birds are there altogether?

You could add them: 4 + 4 + 4 = 12

Or you can multiply: 4 birds × 3 cards = 12 birds

 +  +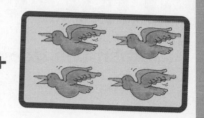

4 + ___ + ___ = ___

___ × 4 = ___

 +

 +

5 + ___ + ___ + ___ = ___

4 × ___ = ___

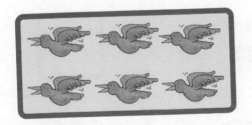 +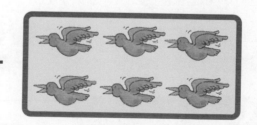

6 + ___ = ___

2 × ___ = ___

Harvest Times

Finish the **addition sentences**.

Addition and
multiplication

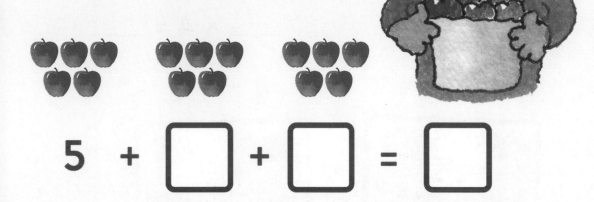

5 + ☐ + ☐ = ☐

Another way to write this sentence is like this:

+

+

5

+

☐

+

☐

☐   ☐

BRAIN BOX

Math sentences can be written two ways:

Example: **addition**	
2 + 3 = 5	2 + 3 ___ 5

Example: **multiplication**	
3 x 1 = 3	3 x 1 ___ 3

We can write the same equation as a **multiplication sentence**.

$$3 \times \boxed{} = \boxed{}$$

We read it aloud as "three times five equals fifteen" or "three groups of five equals fifteen."

Addition and multiplication

We can write the **multiplication sentence** this way too.

Rewrite the **addition sentence** as a **multiplication sentence**.

$$6 + 6 + 6 = \boxed{}$$

$$3 \times \boxed{} = \boxed{}$$

Balloons!

Solve each problem.

Find the **addition** balloon that matches the **multiplication** balloon. Color it the same color.

Addition and multiplication

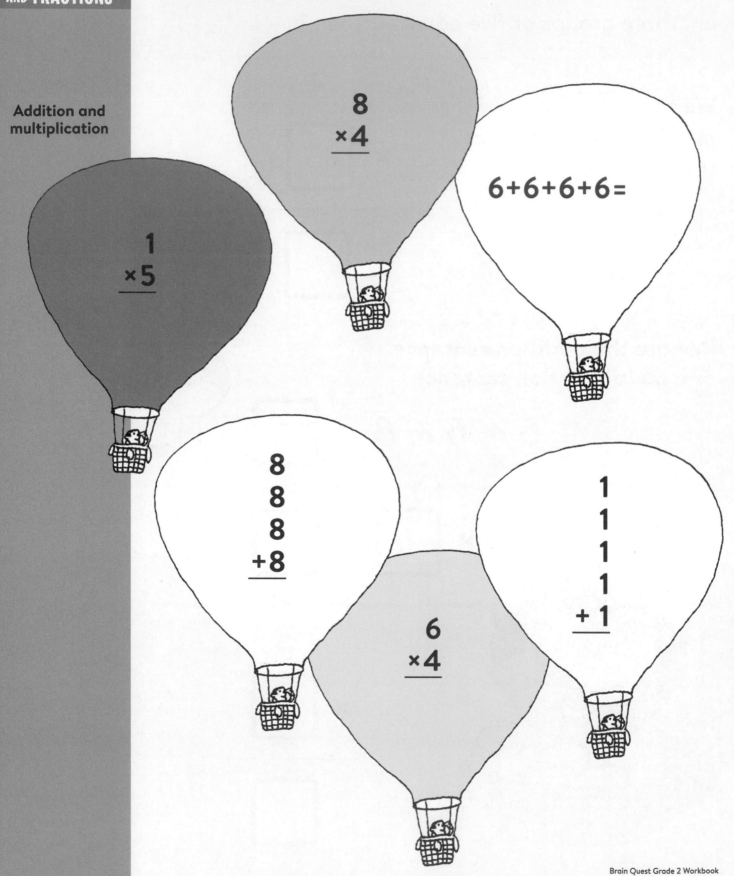

$$8 \times 4$$

$$6+6+6+6=$$

$$1 \times 5$$

$$\begin{array}{r} 8 \\ 8 \\ 8 \\ +8 \\ \hline \end{array}$$

$$6 \times 4$$

$$\begin{array}{r} 1 \\ 1 \\ 1 \\ +1 \\ \hline \end{array}$$

Brain Quest Grade 2 Workbook

Time to Multiply

Multiply. Color each box yellow that equals less than 12.

Multiplication practice

$4 \times 4 =$ _____	$3 \times 2 =$ _____	$5 \times 4 =$ _____
$5 \times 5 =$ _____	$2 \times 2 =$ _____	$3 \times 5 =$ _____
$3 \times 3 =$ _____	$4 \times 1 =$ _____	$0 \times 5 =$ _____
$2 \times 1 =$ _____	$5 \times 2 =$ _____	$8 \times 1 =$ _____
$5 \times 3 =$ _____	$2 \times 0 =$ _____	$4 \times 5 =$ _____
$4 \times 3 =$ _____	$3 \times 3 =$ _____	$3 \times 5 =$ _____

What math symbol did you color? _____

What does the symbol tell you to do? _____

Table Times 10

Write the missing numbers in the **times table**.

MULTIPLICATION AND FRACTIONS

Times table

×	0	1	2	3	4	5	6	7	8	9	10
0	0	0	0	0	0	0	0	0	0	0	0
1	0	1	2	3		5	6	7	8	9	10
2		2	4	6	8	10		14	16	18	20
3	0	3	6	9	12		18	21	24		30
4	0		8	12	16	20	24		32	36	40
5	0	5		15	20	25	30	35	40	45	
6		6	12	18	24	30	36	42		54	60
7	0	7	14		28	35		49	56	63	70
8	0	8		24	32	40	48		64	72	80
9	0	9	18	27		45	54	63	72	81	90
10	0	10	20		40	50	60	70		90	100

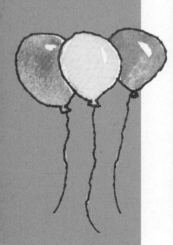

BRAIN BOX

A **factor** is a number that is multiplied in a multiplication equation.

The **product** is the answer in a multiplication equation.

Example: 5 × 4 = 20

The 5 and 4 are factors.
20 is the product.

Use the **times table** to help you answer the questions.

Benito has 4 bags of marbles. There are 6 marbles in each bag. How many marbles does Benito have?

__4__ × __6__ = __24__ marbles

Julia tied 1 balloon to the back of each chair. There are 8 chairs at the table. How many balloons does Julia need?

_____ × _____ = _____ balloons

Dad filled the washing machines with towels. Each machine holds 5 towels. Dad used 3 machines. How many towels did he wash?

_____ × _____ = _____ towels

Mom and Sis are hanging wallpaper. They have 3 rooms to do. Each room will need 9 rolls of wallpaper. How many rolls of wallpaper do they need to do all 3 rooms?

_____ × _____ = _____ rolls of wallpaper

Each horse in the barn eats 3 buckets of oats every day. How many buckets of oats are needed to feed 4 horses?

_____ × _____ = _____ buckets

$\frac{1}{2}$ **Equals One-Half**

Color **one-half** of each shape.
Write the **fraction** in the space you colored.

Fractions

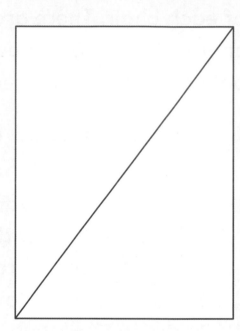

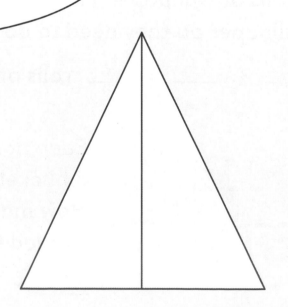

BRAIN BOX

Fractions show parts of a whole.

They can be written in words (**one-half**) or numbers ($\frac{1}{2}$).

If you take one shape and cut it into two equal parts, each part is $\frac{1}{2}$ of the shape.

$\frac{1}{4}$ Equals One-Quarter

Color **one-quarter**, or **one-fourth**, of each shape.
Write the **fraction** in the space you colored.

Fractions

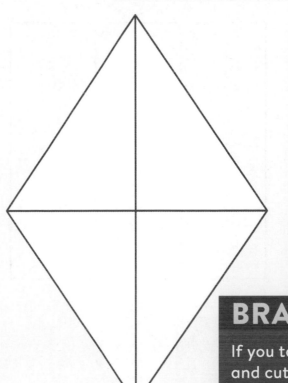

BRAIN BOX

If you take one shape and cut it into four equal parts, each part is $\frac{1}{4}$ of the shape.

Fractions

⅓ Equals One-Third

Color **one-third** of each shape.

Write the **fraction** in the space you colored.

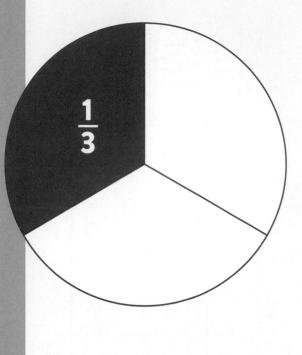

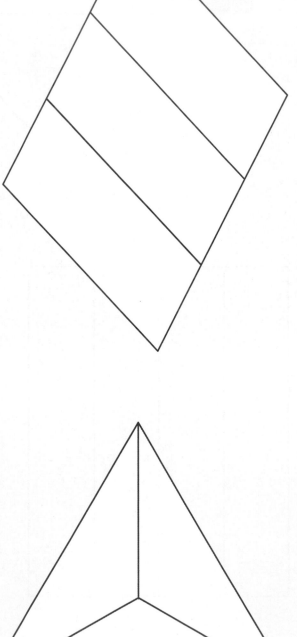

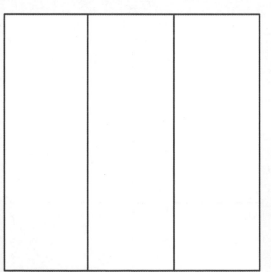

BRAIN BOX

If you take one shape and cut it into three equal parts, each part is $\frac{1}{3}$ of the shape.

A Piece of Pie

Draw a line from the **fraction** to the matching shape.

Matching fractions

$\frac{1}{2}$  $\frac{1}{4}$  $\frac{1}{3}$  $\frac{2}{4}$

Color in the fractions below.

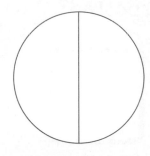

Color $\frac{1}{2}$ red.

Color $\frac{2}{3}$ blue.

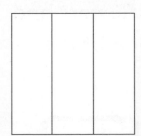

Color $\frac{1}{3}$ green.

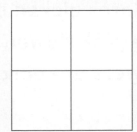

Color $\frac{1}{4}$ yellow.

Word Problems

Read each problem.

Write the answer in **words** on the line.

Write the answer as a **fraction** in the box.

Fractions and
word problems

Ian cut his muffin in half. If he eats half of the muffin, how much will he have left to give to his little brother?

_____

Fred's dog Daisy just had three puppies! One puppy is pure black. The other two are brown with little black spots. What fraction of the puppies are spotted?

_____

Dolores picked three yellow flowers and one pink flower. What fraction of the flowers are pink?

_____

SHAPES AND MEASUREMENT

Do you know how many inches tall you are? What about your favorite toy—how tall is that? Keep an eye out for different measuring tools, like a ruler, a measuring cup, or a scale, and start measuring!

PARENTS Exploring three-dimensional shapes and measurement tools, such as scales and rulers, will help your child build geometry skills. Concepts in this section are ideal for hands-on practice around the home. Let your child use playdough or building blocks to make shapes and then measure them!

PLACE A STICKER HERE

Name That Shape!

Read the clues.

Write the names of the **shapes**.

I have four sides. Two of my sides are short. Two are long.

What am I? ___rectangle___

I have no sides at all. I go round and round.

What am I? _____

I have four sides. Each side is the same length.

What am I? _____

I have four sides. You can find me in a deck of cards or on a baseball field.

What am I? _____

I have three sides.

What am I? _____

Same Shape

Look at the shape on the top card.

Draw a matching shape on the card below.

Two-dimensional shapes

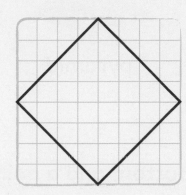

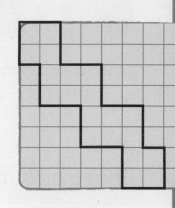

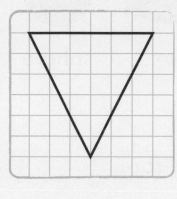

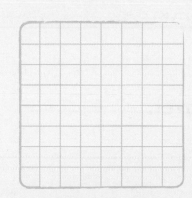

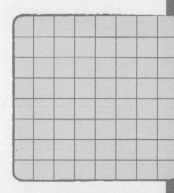

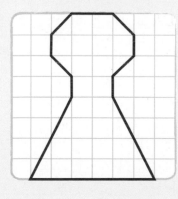

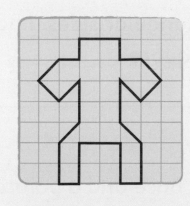

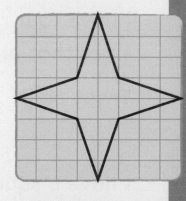

216

SHAPES AND
MEASUREMENT

Three-
dimensional
shapes

Geometry Mystery

Read the clues.
Write the names of the shapes.

cube   cone   pyramid   box   sphere

I have a round bottom and a pointed top.

What am I? _cone_____

I am round all over.

What am I? _____

I have four rectangular sides. I have two
sides that are square.

What am I? _____

I have a square base and a pointed top.

What am I? _____

I have six square sides.

What am I? _____

Made to Measure

Choose the correct word from the boxes below to complete each sentence.

weight	length
volume	temperature

Measurement tools

We use a **measuring cup** to measure

_____.

We use a **ruler** to measure

_____.

We use a **thermometer** to measure

_____.

We use a **scale** to measure

_____.

Measure It!

Write the **weight** of each basket of fruit.

Then answer the questions.

_____ pounds   _____ pounds

To measure the water in a bathtub, would you use
a **cup** or a **gallon jug**?

_____

To measure the distance from your room to the
kitchen, would you use **feet** or **miles**?

_____

If the thermometer reads 35°F, would you wear a
swimsuit or a **snowsuit**?

_____

Inch by Inch

Cut out the **ruler** along the dotted line.

Use it to measure the pictures.

Then complete the sentences.

Save your ruler to use for the next four pages.

Measuring with a ruler

 The quarter is ____1____ inch wide.

The teaspoon is _____ inches long.

BRAIN BOX

To use your Brain Quest ruler, put the red start edge at one end of the object you want to measure.

See where the end of the object lines up with the ruler. That number is your final meaasurement.

The toy car is _____ inches long.

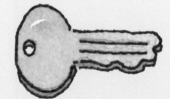 The key is _____ inches long.

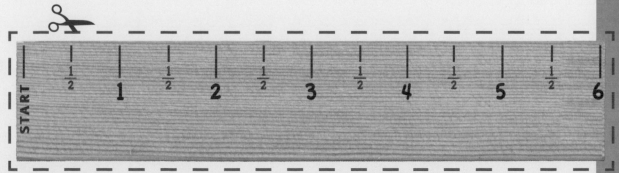

Hand-y Measurements

Put one hand in the frame. Spread your fingers apart.

Use a pencil to trace around your fingers and hand.

Write which hand you traced on the frame.

Measuring with a ruler

My _____ Hand

Measure your hand with the ruler from page 219.

Write the measurements to the nearest inch or half inch on the lines.

Measuring with a ruler

My hand is about _____ inches long.

My hand is about _____ inches wide.

My thumb is about _____ inches long.

My pointer finger is about _____ inches long.

My middle finger is about _____ inches long.

My ring finger is about _____ inches long.

My pinkie is about _____ inches long.

BRAIN BOX

Length measures how long or tall something is.

Width measures how wide something is.

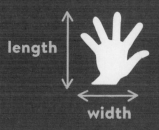

The Right Size

Measure these things you can find in your home.

My favorite toy is _____ inches long.

My favorite book is _____ inches long and _____ inches wide.

A roll of toilet paper is _____ inches long and _____ inches wide.

A marker is _____ inches long.

An apple is _____ inches long.

A mug is _____ inches deep.

My toothbrush is _____ inches long.

TIME AND MONEY

What time is it now? Do you know the names of these coins and how much they're worth? Turn the page to learn more about time and money!

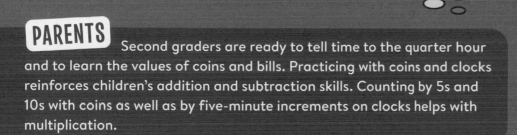

PARENTS Second graders are ready to tell time to the quarter hour and to learn the values of coins and bills. Practicing with coins and clocks reinforces children's addition and subtraction skills. Counting by 5s and 10s with coins as well as by five-minute increments on clocks helps with multiplication.

PLACE A STICKER HERE

For additional resources, visit www.BrainQuest.com/grade2

On the hour

What Time Is It?

Find the two clocks that match the words.

Draw lines between the words and the matching clocks.

10:00

one o'clock

nine o'clock

ten o'clock

five o'clock

two o'clock

1:00

9:00

5:00

2:00

BRAIN BOX

An analog clock has three parts:

1. A clock face.

2. A little hand that points to the hour.

3. A big hand that points to the minute.

big hand

little hand

This clock says that it is 3 o'clock.

A digital clock shows the time in numbers:

This clock says it is 3 o'clock too.

3:00

Draw the missing hour hand to show the time.

2:00

10:00

5:00

7:00

Half Past

Color the clocks that show **half past** the hour.

Half hours

Draw the missing minute hand to show the time.

5:30   7:30   1:30   4:30

BRAIN BOX

One hour equals **60** minutes.

Half an hour equals **30** minutes.

Look at this clock:

The minute hand is pointing to the 6. This means it's **30** minutes after the hour, or **half past the hour.**

This clock says it's **half past 12,** or **12:30.**

15 Minutes Before and After

Find the clock faces that show a **quarter past** the hour. Color them yellow.

Find the clock faces that show a **quarter to** the hour. Color them blue.

Quarter hours

BRAIN BOX

A quarter hour is **15** minutes.

Look at this clock:

The minute hand is pointing to the **3**. This means it's **15** minutes after the hour, or a **quarter past**.

The clock says it's a **quarter past 1** or **1:15**.

Now look at this clock:

The minute hand is pointing to the **9**. This means it's **45** minutes after the hour, or **1:45**.

It also means that it is **15** minutes to the next hour, or a **quarter to 2:00**.

Draw the missing minute hand to show the time.

12:15   **11:45**   **5:45**   **8:15**

It's Getting Late!

Draw the minute hand to show the time on the hour.

Write the missing times on the lines.

One hour later

1:00   2:00   3:00   _____

5:00   7:00   _____

What time is it right now?

Write the time on the line.

Draw the clock hands.

_____

What time will it be in an hour?

Write the time on the line.

Draw the clock hands.

_____

My Times

Write the time on the **digital** clock.

Then draw the clock hands to show the same time on the **analog** clock.

Daily schedule

I wake up at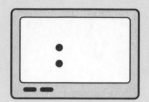

I go to school at

I come home at

I eat dinner at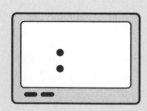

I go to bed at

Tell the Time

Write the time below each clock.

Telling time

12:45

_____   _____   _____

_____   _____   _____   _____

_____   _____   _____   _____

Money Riddles

Read the clues and questions.

Circle the answers.

I am worth 5 pennies. Two of me make a dime.
What am I?

How many cents am I worth?

1¢   5¢   10¢   25¢

I am the smallest-sized coin. But I am worth
more than a nickel or a penny.
What am I?

How many cents am I worth?

1¢   5¢   10¢   25¢

TIME AND MONEY

Penny, nickel,
dime, quarter

BRAIN BOX

 penny = 1¢

 nickel = 5¢

 dime = 10¢

 quarter = 25¢

Penny, nickel, dime, quarter

I am not silver. You need 100 of me to make a dollar. What am I?

How many cents am I worth?

1¢   5¢   10¢   25¢

I am one-fourth of a dollar. I am worth 5 nickels or 2 dimes and 5 pennies.
What am I?

How many cents am I worth?

1¢   5¢   10¢   25¢

Fruit Stand

Circle the exact change needed to buy each fruit.
Then count the change left over.

How much money is left? ___28¢___

How much money is left? _____

How much money is left? _____

76¢

How much money is left? _____

Count the money.

81¢

How much more money would
you need to buy the oranges? _____

What coins would make up that amount?

_____

Got Change?

How many of each coin equal a **dollar**?

Write the missing numbers in the chart.

Change for
a dollar

BRAIN BOX

This is a dollar bill.

It is worth **100 cents.**
$1.00 = 100¢

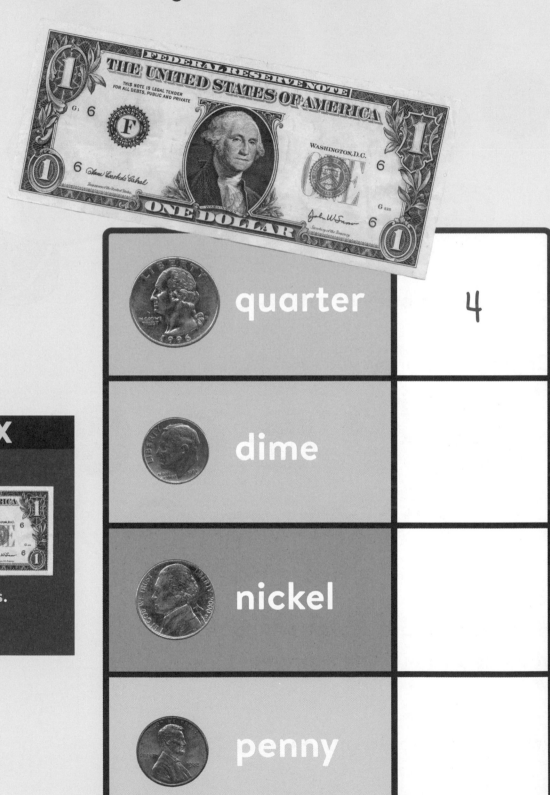

quarter	4
dime	
nickel	
penny	

Even Steven

How many equal the same amount of money?

 = _____5_____ ×

 = _____ ×

 = _____ ×

 = _____ ×

 = _____ ×

Brain Quest Grade 2 Workbook

Which Is More?

Add the coins.

Write the amount on the line.

Compare the coins to the dollar bill or bills.

Circle the **greater** amount.

Adding money

Total ___85¢___

Total _____

Adding
money

Total _____

Total _____

Piggy Bank

Draw a line from each group of coins to the matching piggy bank.

Adding money

SOCIAL STUDIES

Did you know that social studies is about so much more than maps and important cities? In this section, we'll learn about historic and current people, places, and holidays.

PARENTS Social studies encompasses topics from government and economics to geography, culture, and history. Second graders can be very curious about where they live and what life was like in the past. Help connect the world around them and the people in it to your child's life and experiences.

PLACE A
STICKER
HERE

Map It!

Use the **map key** to label the continents.

Reading
a map

Map Key

North America

South America

Europe

Asia

Australia

Africa

Antarctica

BRAIN BOX

A **map** of the world is a picture of the Earth's surface.

A **compass** shows the four directions: **north, south, east, west.**

A **key** or **legend** explains the small pictures or symbols on the map.

Reading
a map

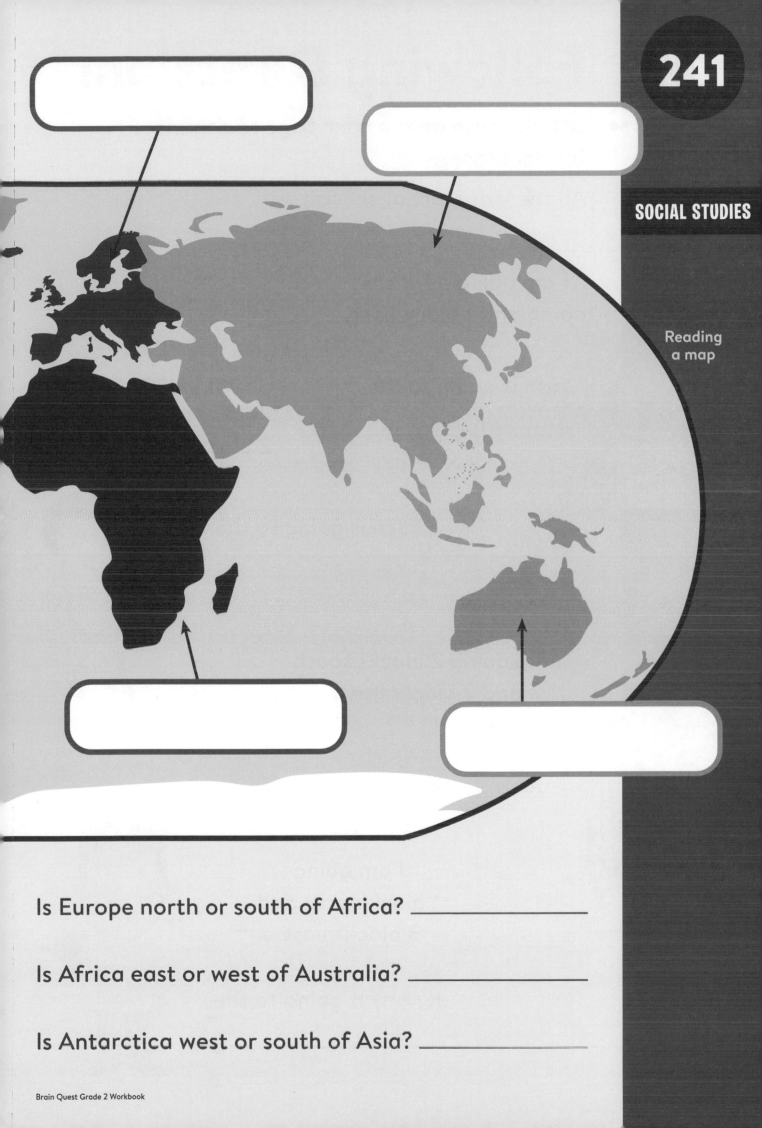

Is Europe north or south of Africa? _____

Is Africa east or west of Australia? _____

Is Antarctica west or south of Asia? _____

Following Directions

Use the **map** on the next page to complete the sentences.

All the kids start at school.

Map practice

I am going 4 blocks north and 1 block east.

Josh is going to the

_____ .

I am going 2 blocks south and 2 blocks west.

Jen is going to the

_____ .

I am going 2 blocks south and 2 blocks east.

Jane is going to the _____ .

I am going 1 block north and 3 blocks east.

Jeremy is going to the

_____ .

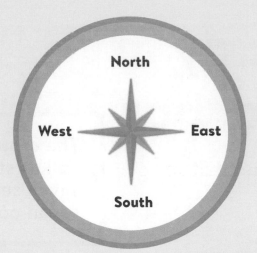

				music school		
post office						
						library
			school			
	ball field				market	
	play-ground					

The Lady in the Harbor

Read about the Statue of Liberty.

National monument

The **crown** with seven **spikes** stands for the seven seas and the seven continents.

The **torch** is a light that welcomes travelers to the United States.

JULY IV

The **foot's forward position** is a symbol of moving forward into the future.

The **tablet** shows the Roman numerals of the date the Declaration of Independence was signed: July 4, 1776.

The Statue of Liberty stands on an island in New York Harbor. She is a symbol of freedom and hope.

Liberty means freedom, the ability to act and think as you want. This can look like voting for the candidate you like the most or celebrating the holidays that are important to your family. What does liberty mean to you?

Write a poem about liberty.

Begin the first word of each line with the letter shown.

L _____

I _____

B _____

E _____

R _____

T _____

Y _____

National monument

Calendar Crunch

Write the months of the year in order on the **time line**.

Use the month names in the boxes.

April
August
December
February
January
July
June
March
May
November
October
September

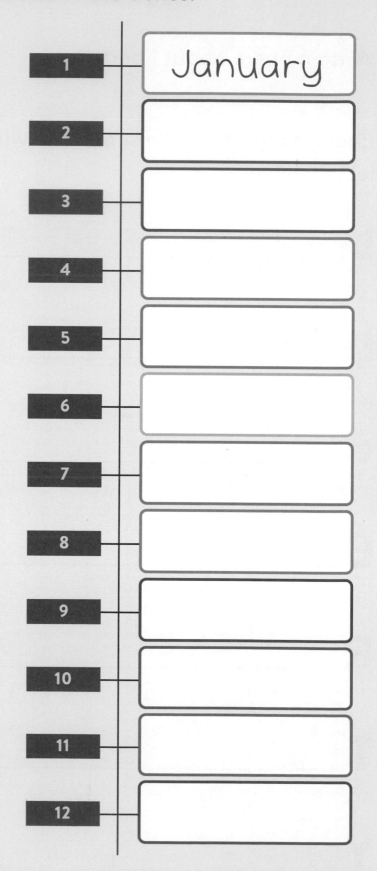

1 January
2
3
4
5
6
7
8
9
10
11
12

List the birthdays and holidays you celebrate on the calendar below.

Time line

January	February	March

April	May	June

July	August	September

October	November	December

Transportation Time Line

Today, there are many ways to travel, but there were not as many options in the past. Read about the different kinds of transportation people have used over the years, then fill in the blanks on the time line.

Past, present, and future

Long ago
Long ago, if you wanted to travel to visit friends and family, you had to put on your walking shoes or saddle up your **horse** . . . or your mule, donkey, or camel.

1804
British engineer and inventor Richard Trevithick pioneered the first **steam train** in 1804. During the 1800s, more trains and routes were built, allowing people to travel farther and faster than they could before.

1885
The first **automobile** was designed by German Karl Benz in 1885. It had only three wheels! In 1913, the Ford Model T became the first automobile to be built on an assembly line, making cars cheaper and available to more people.

| horse | | | | | | |

| 1780 | 1800 | 1820 | 1840 | 1860 | 1880 | 1900 |

1903
The brothers Orville and Wilbur Wright made the first successful **airplane** flight in 1903. Since then, many different kinds of aircraft have been developed to fly people and cargo around the world.

Think about an invention people might use for travel in the future! In the "Future" box, draw a sketch of your invention and write about how it works. Then add it to the timeline!

Today
Many people drive **hybrid cars,** which have both gasoline engines and electric motors, and **electric vehicles,** which run on rechargeable batteries. These cars produce less air pollution than gasoline-powered cars.

Future

| 1940 | 1960 | 1980 | 2000 | 2020 | 2040 | 2060 |

hybrid and electric vehicles

Marching for Justice

Read about Martin Luther King Jr.

Civil rights

Dr. Martin Luther King Jr. was a minister, a civil rights leader, and a champion for racial justice. He believed that all people should be treated fairly and that harmful and unfair laws should be changed. Dr. King made speeches and helped organize marches to protest segregation, a practice of keeping groups of people separate because of the color of their skin.

On August 28, 1963, 250,000 people came to Washington, DC, for the March on Washington for Jobs and Freedom to support the cause of civil rights. Here, Dr. King gave his famous "I Have a Dream" speech. This is part of Dr. King's speech from that day:

"I have a dream . . . a dream that my four little children will one day live in a nation where they will not be judged by the color of their skin but by the content of their character."

Dr. King's birthday is celebrated across the United States on the third Monday in January.

Is there something that you think is unfair in our world today? Is there something you think we should fight for? Write your own speech about this below.

I believe that _____

_____

_____

_____

_____

_____

_____

_____

_____

_____

_____

_____

_____

Civil rights

Big Birthdays

Read about George Washington and Abraham Lincoln to complete the crossword puzzle.

Washington Monument

George Washington and Abraham Lincoln were born in the month of February. Both presidents have monuments in our nation's capital, Washington, DC. Each year, we celebrate their lives and achievements on Presidents' Day, the third Monday in February.

George Washington was the first president of the United States, from 1789 to 1797. He was born on February 22, 1732, in Virginia. The Washington Monument honors Washington's life. It is a tall stone obelisk. An obelisk is a four-sided stone tower. Inside, 897 steps take visitors to a room near the top. What a view!

Abraham Lincoln was the sixteenth president of the United States, from 1861 to 1865. He was born on February 12, 1809, in Kentucky. The Lincoln Memorial looks like a Greek temple. It is a building with three rooms. A statue of Abraham Lincoln sits in the center room.

Lincoln Memorial

Presidents'
Day

Across

2. The Lincoln __ __ __ __ __ __ __ __ has three rooms.

4. The national holiday celebrated on the third Monday in February is __ __ __ __ __ __ __ __ __ __ __' Day.

6. The Washington __ __ __ __ __ __ __ __ __ is a tall tower.

Down

1. George Washington was the __ __ __ __ __ president.

3. Washington, DC, is the __ __ __ __ __ __ __ __ of the United States.

5. The 16th president was Abraham __ __ __ __ __ __ __ .

Independence Day

Read about the Fourth of July.

We celebrate America's birthday on the fourth day of July. The Fourth of July is also called Independence Day.

On July 4, 1776, the Continental Congress met in Philadelphia, Pennsylvania, and adopted the Declaration of Independence. This paper said that America was no longer ruled by England. It declared America free! The Declaration is still a symbol of American liberty. We celebrate what it stands for every Fourth of July.

We celebrate this holiday in many different ways.
To find out how, unscramble each word.

FIOKWERSR <u>fireworks</u>

LGAF _ _ _ _

TCONREC _ _ _ _ _ _ _

PRADEA _ _ _ _ _ _

Celebrating Freedom

Read about Juneteenth.

Juneteenth is a holiday celebrating the end of slavery in the United States. During the Civil War, President Abraham Lincoln issued the Emancipation Proclamation on January 1, 1863, which freed enslaved people in rebelling confederate states. But the proclamation was difficult to enforce, and many people remained enslaved until after the war ended in 1865. On June 19, 1865, Union troops reached Galveston Bay, Texas and freed the last enslaved people there. This day, June 19, is known as Juneteenth.

Juneteenth

What does freedom mean to you? Write about it below.

_____

_____

_____

_____

_____

_____

BRAIN BOX

During the **American Civil War** (1861–1865), Northern and Southern states went to war over slavery. Lawmakers in the Northern states, known as the Union, wanted to abolish (end) slavery throughout the country. Lawmakers in the Southern states wanted to keep slavery legal, so they decided to leave the United States and start a new government called the Confederacy.

Famous Americans

Read about these important Americans.

Write their names and birth years in order on the time line below.

Historical figures

Orville Wright (born 1871) and Wilbur Wright (born 1867)

Together, the Wright brothers invented the airplane. On December 17, 1903, Orville flew the plane above Kitty Hawk, North Carolina. Although he flew only 120 feet and for just 12 seconds, it began the age of air travel.

Red Cloud (born 1822)

Born in what is today Nebraska, Red Cloud was a leader of the Oglala Lakota people. He led the fight against the US government's attempts to take his people's land. In 1870 and 1875, Red Cloud met with President Ulysses S. Grant to speak up for the rights of Indigenous Americans.

Helen Keller (born 1880)

Helen Keller lost her ability to see and hear after a childhood illness. She communicated with home signs until a teacher named Anne Sulllivan taught her how to read, write, and use sign language. Keller was the first person who was deaf and blind to earn a college degree and went on to become a famous writer and activist.

1790	1800	1810	1820	1830	1840

Historical
figures

Jane Addams (born 1860)

Jane Addams fought for peace and women's rights. In 1889, she opened a place called Hull House, in Chicago, Illinois. At Hull House, people in need could find help with education and child care. Jane Addams was the first American woman to be awarded the Nobel Peace Prize in 1931.

Sojourner Truth (born 1797)

Sojourner Truth was a Black woman who worked to end slavery and improve women's rights. Born an enslaved person, she escaped later in her life and lived as a free woman. She argued that Black soldiers should be part of the Union army during the Civil War. President Abraham Lincoln invited her to the White House.

Frederick Douglass (born 1818)

Born an enslaved person in Maryland, Frederick Douglass escaped to New York in 1838. He became a leader in the movement to end slavery. He traveled the country talking about his experiences as an enslaved person. In 1845, he published a famous book about his life. He became an advisor to President Abraham Lincoln during the Civil War. He spent his entire life fighting for Black Americans to have more rights.

| 1850 | 1860 | 1870 | 1880 | 1890 | 1900 |

Orville Wright, 1871

Historical figures

Jonas Salk (born 1914)

Polio is a very dangerous disease with no cure. In the early 1900s, thousands of people got very sick or died from it every year. Jonas Salk was a doctor who developed a vaccine for polio in 1955. Because of his vaccine, polio did not appear in the US from 1979 to 2022.

Cesar Chavez (born 1927) and Dolores Huerta (born 1930)

Cesar Chavez was a Mexican American labor rights leader. He organized workers to create unions and to demand fair treatment and fair pay at work. In 1962, he and labor leader Dolores Huerta started a union called the United Farm Workers of America. Their work led to better conditions and pay for migrant workers.

Amelia Earhart (born 1897)

In 1932, Amelia Earhart became the first woman—and only the second person ever—to fly nonstop across the Atlantic Ocean alone. In 1935, after flying from Hawaii to California, she became the first person to fly solo across both the Atlantic *and* Pacific Oceans.

1890   1900   1910

Historical
figures

Thurgood Marshall (born 1908)

Thurgood Marshall was the first Black justice on the US Supreme Court. As a civil rights lawyer he won a case called *Brown v. Board of Education*, which ruled that segregation in public schools is unequal and illegal. This decision helped advance the civil rights movement in America.

Rosa Parks (born 1913)

On December 1, 1955, in Montgomery, Alabama, activist Rosa Parks was arrested for refusing to give up her bus seat to a white man. At that time, Black citizens in Alabama were required to sit at the back of the bus and to give up their seats to white passengers. Her brave actions started the Montgomery bus boycott, which ended when the US Supreme Court ruled that segregation on public buses was unconstitutional.

Rachel Carson (born 1907)

Rachel Carson was a writer and scientist who wrote a book called *Silent Spring* in 1962. She warned that chemicals used by farmers to protect food crops from insects were dangerous to wildlife, the environment, and humans. Carson's book helped start the environmental movement, which works to protect the natural world.

1920   1930   1940

Dolores Huerta, 1930

My Time Line!

Fill in the time line with important events, starting with the year you were born.

What will your future hold? Imagine it, then fill in all the important events of your life!

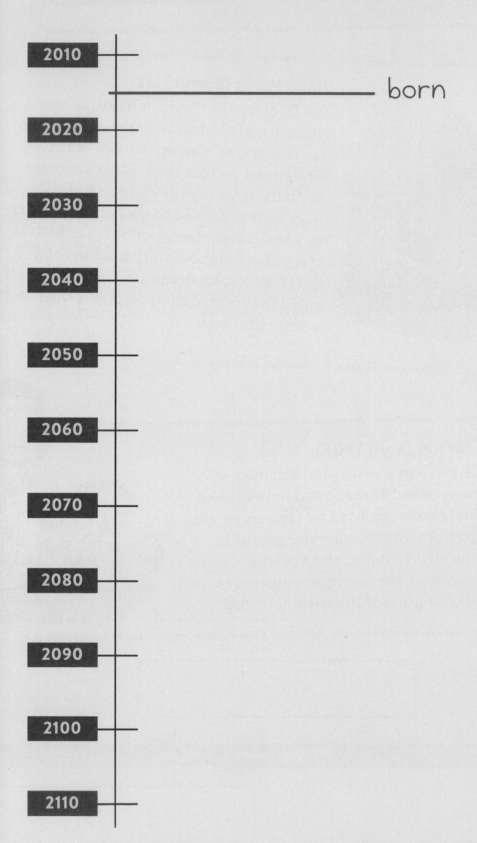

2010

_____ born

2020

2030

2040

2050

2060

2070

2080

2090

2100

2110

SCIENCE

Do you like to ask questions? If so, you'll make a great scientist! Scientists ask questions to understand how the world works. Ready to learn more? Let's dig in!

PARENTS Explore concepts of earth, life, and physical science that are foundational to science learning throughout school. Help your learner to think like a scientist. Let them ask questions that go beyond the content of these pages. And if you can't answer their question, it's great to say, "I don't know, but let's find out!"

Landforms

Look at the picture.

Label the different **landforms** and **bodies of water** using the words from the boxes.

Land	Water
volcano	lake
mountains	inlet
plateau	river
island	

BRAIN BOX

Landforms are natural features on Earth's surface, like mountains and canyons.

Bodies of water are areas of Earth's surface covered with water, like lakes and oceans.

Water Everywhere!

Read about water.

Liquid

Water is a liquid. Liquid water is wet. Rivers, ponds, lakes, and the sea have liquid water. Clouds are made of tiny water droplets.

Gas

Water is a gas. The gas form is called water vapor. Water vapor is part of the air. When the air feels damp or moist, the air has lots of water vapor in it. Steam is hot water vapor. Fog is cool water vapor.

Solid

Solid water is ice. A snowflake is made up of ice crystals. Ice cubes and icebergs are water in solid form.

Write **liquid**, **gas**, or **solid** under each picture.

solid

_____

_____

_____

_____

Solid, Liquid, or Gas?

Look at each picture. Is it showing a **solid**, a **liquid**, or a **gas**?

liquid

_____

_____

_____

_____

_____

_____

_____   _____

Write the name of each solid, liquid, or gas under the correct heading on the chart.

Solid	Liquid	Gas
	ketchup	

Energy to Grow

Read about **photosynthesis**.

Your body needs energy to play. You get energy from the food you eat. Plants need energy to grow too. Plants get the energy they need from sunlight. Plants use air, water, and sunlight to make their own food. A green substance in plants called chlorophyll [KLOR-uh-fil] absorbs sunlight and makes plants green. Inside plants, the chlorophyll uses the light energy and air to make the food plants need to grow. This process is called photosynthesis [foh-toh-SIN-thuh-sis].

BRAIN BOX

An **experiment** is a test to try to find out about something.

Read about a photosynthesis experiment.

Number the pictures to show the correct order of the steps.

Photosynthesis

1. A plant uses sunlight to make food. A healthy plant is green.

2. Cover one leaf with foil.

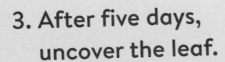

3. After five days, uncover the leaf.

Complete the sentence:

The leaf turned yellow because it didn't get the

_____ it needed

to make it green.

How Do Plants Grow?

All plants need sunlight, water, and nutrients from soil to live and grow.

Where will a plant grow better? Circle your answer.

under a shady tree **OR** in direct sunlight?

in a rainy plain **OR** in a desert?

in soil with many **OR** in soil with no
nutrients nutrients?

in a cave **OR** on a grassy hill?

on a glacier **OR** on a tropical island?

Pollinating Plants

Read the text below. Then answer the questions about **pollination**.

Pollination

Pollinate means to move pollen from one plant to another. Bees, butterflies, birds, and other animals pollinate plants.

When an animal stops to feed at a flower, some of the flower's pollen grains stick to the animal. When the animal moves on to feed at another plant, it takes these pollen grains with it. This moves pollen around from plant to plant.

Wind and water can also pollinate by moving pollen grains from one plant to another.

Circle the correct answer. **Pollinate** means to:

| Eat pollen grains | Move pollen grains from one plant to another | Fly by a plant quickly |

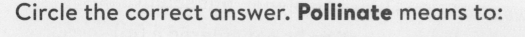

Name two animals that are pollinators.

_____

Why do we need pollinators?

BRAIN BOX

Pollen is powdery and found inside flowering plants. Pollen grains allow plants to reproduce, or make more plants.

_____

Address: Earth

Read about Earth and circle it in the picture below.

You live in a home on a street or road.

Your street or road is in a town or city.

Your town or city is in a state.

Your state is in a country.

Your country is on a continent.

Your continent is on the planet Earth.

And where is Earth?

Earth is in the solar system. It is one of eight planets in our solar system that orbit (circle around) the sun. Pluto was once considered a planet, but scientists decided that it's too small to be considered a full planet. Pluto is now called a dwarf planet.

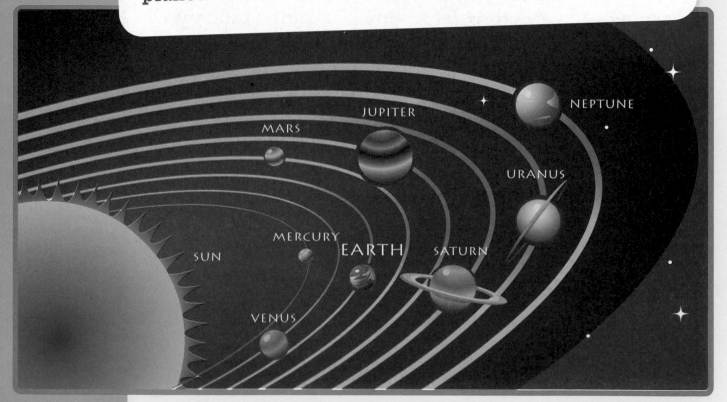

Use the picture to answer the questions.

List the eight planets that orbit the sun.

M _Mercury_

V _____

E _____

M _____

J _____

S _____

U _____

N _____

BRAIN BOX

You can recall the order of the planets with a mnemonic (pronounced ni-mon-ik), a tool that helps you remember: My Very Excellent Mother Just Served Us Noodles.

Which planet is closest to the sun?

_____

Which planet is farthest from the sun?

_____

Which two planets are Earth's closest neighbors?

_____

Stay Healthy!

Maiko loves to jump rope to stay healthy.

She made a **chart** to keep track of how long she jumps rope each day.

Use her chart to answer the questions.

CHART	
Day	**Minutes**
Mon.	15
Tues.	10
Wed.	20
Thurs.	12
Fri.	18
Sat.	18
Sun.	13

On which day did Maiko exercise the most?

_____

On which day did she exercise the least?

_____

On which two days did she exercise
the same amount of time?

_____

Use the chart to complete the **graph** for Thursday through Sunday. Color in each box until you reach the number of minutes for each day.

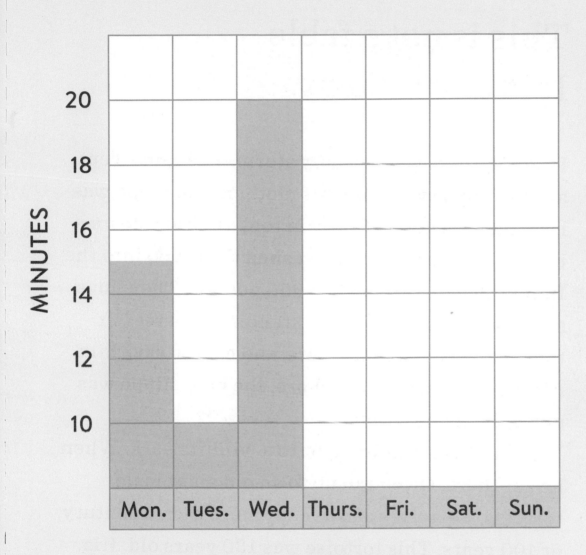

How do **you** exercise to stay healthy?

_____

_____

The Hippo and the Tortoise

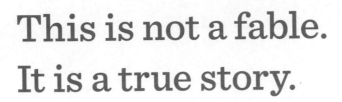

Read the story.

This is not a fable. It is a true story.

In 2004, there was a deadly storm. The rain swept a baby hippo away from his mother. The hippo was less than a year old. The rain took the baby down a river in Kenya. The river washed the hippo into the Indian Ocean. He weighed 650 pounds. Then huge storm waves left the hippo standing on a reef. It took many boats, ropes, nets, and cars to save him. After he was brought to shore, the baby hippo was given the name Owen.

Then Owen was brought to a wildlife park. When he got there, Owen ran up to an old giant male tortoise. Tortoises can live for more than a century, or 100 years. This tortoise was 130 years old. His name was Mzee. Owen and Mzee liked to swim, eat, and sleep side by side. Owen followed Mzee the same way he would have followed his mother. Hippos stay with their moms for about four years. Owen had a new "mother."

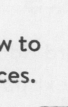

Use words from below to complete the sentences.

| Kenya | rough | oceans | years | fable |

This story is not a ___ ___ ___ ___ .

The waves were ___ ___ ___ .

Atlantic, Pacific, and Indian are names of

___ ___ ___ ___ .

This happened in ___ ___ ___ ___ .

A century is 100 ___ ___ ___ .

Write the letters from the colored boxes in the matching boxes below to complete the sentence.

Owen is one  hippo!

Bird Riddles

Draw a line from each bird riddle on this page to the correct bird on the next page.

My tail is so beautiful! I can fly, but I would rather walk and strut. What am I?

I have feathers and a beak, and I lay eggs like other birds. But I do not fly through the air. I fly through the water! What am I?

I am a beautiful bird too! I have a sharp beak. If you are patient, you might be able to teach me to say, "Polly want a cracker." What am I?

I am tall. I have a long neck. My feathers are pink from the pink shrimp I like to eat. What am I?

I am a small bird. The feathers on my chest are red. You see me in the spring. What am I?

I have a red comb on top of my head. In the early morning you might hear me call, "cock-a-doodle-do!" What am I?

SCIENCE

Birds

Land and sea mammals

The Camel's a Mammal

Read about **mammals**.

Mammals:

✓ breathe air through lungs.

✓ are born alive. They do not hatch.

✓ drink milk their mothers make.

✓ have hair. Some are born with hair and lose it as they grow up.

Circle all the mammals.

Most mammals live on land, but some mammals live in the sea.

Sea mammals have lungs. They swim up to the surface to breathe air.

Sea creatures that are not mammals do not need to breathe air.

Circle the sea creatures that are mammals.

Hey, Shelly!

Read about the snail and the turtle.

Snail

The snail is not a mammal or a reptile. It is a mollusk. The snail's body is soft, but it's protected by a hard shell. How does the snail move? Very slowly! That's because it has just one foot. This soft, flat foot makes a slimy liquid that helps it crawl. A snail has two pairs of tentacles. It sees with eyespots on its long tentacles. The short tentacles help the snail smell and touch.

Painted Turtle

The painted turtle lives in a large group. It lives in slow-moving rivers with soft, muddy bottoms. The turtle is a reptile with a shell. Its hard shell is called a carapace.

When it's cold outside, the turtle hibernates under the mud. A turtle is slow on land, but its webbed feet help it swim. When danger is near, the turtle pulls its head, legs, and tail inside the shell to protect itself.

Write facts about how snails and turtles are the same in the green space.

Write facts about how snails are different in the blue space.

Write facts about how turtles are different in the yellow space.

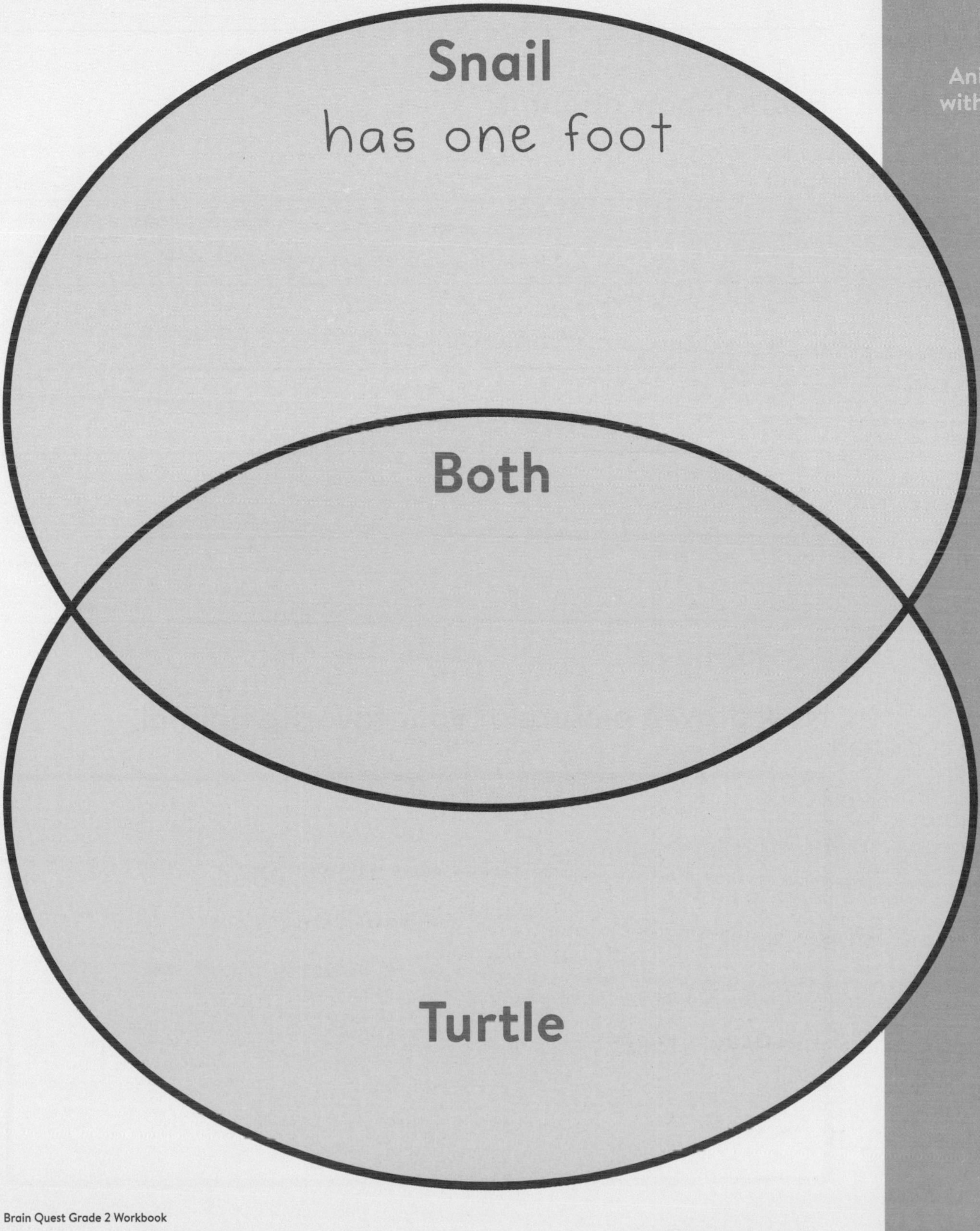

Animals with shells

Snail
has one foot

Both

Turtle

My Favorite Animal

Complete the sentences.

My favorite animal is _____ .

I like it because _____

_____ .

Facts I know about it:

1. _____

_____ .

2. _____

_____ .

3. _____

_____ .

Now draw a picture of your favorite animal.

TECHNOLOGY

Which shape comes next in the pattern?

▲ ▲ ▲ ▲ ▲ ▲ ▲ __

If you can complete the pattern, you can also code! We'll start by learning more about computers, and then we'll learn how to program them.

PARENTS From understanding icons and keystrokes to using coding blocks, second graders are building the foundations of coding. In these exercises, your child will develop logic and problem-solving skills, which are useful in all educational disciplines.

PLACE A STICKER HERE

Icons!

Sometimes a small picture, called an **icon,** can tell us a lot of information. What happens if you click certain pictures on a computer? Draw a line between the icon and what it means or does.

word processor

paint program

cut text or pictures

go to a home page

close a program
or window

turn power on or off

Which Key Am I?

Look at the computer keyboard. Find and color the key for each clue.

Color the key that will erase text **blue**.

Color the very long key that moves the cursor forward one space **red**.

Color the keys that make letters into capitals green.

Color the keys that make the computer sounds louder and softer **purple**.

Color the key that makes the cursor move to the beginning of the next row orange.

BRAIN BOX

A **cursor** is a shape that moves to show where you are working on a screen. It may look like an arrow that you can move with a mouse or trackpad, or it may look like a blinking line that shows where you will be typing.

Turtle Time!

A computer follows instructions called **commands.** Here are some commands you could use to make a robot move.

To move forward one step: MOVE FORWARD

To turn right: TURN RIGHT

To turn left: TURN LEFT

To make a robot move forward two steps and then turn right, you would write:

MOVE FORWARD

MOVE FORWARD

TURN RIGHT

Draw a path below to help the turtle robot reach the finish line. Remember to pay attention to the direction the turtle is facing!

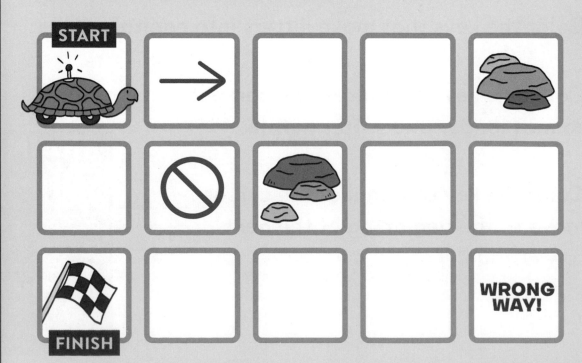

Write the steps the turtle should take to reach the finish line. Remember to pay attention to the direction the turtle is facing! **Hint:** It should take ten steps!

MOVE FORWARD

TURN RIGHT

TURN LEFT

MOVE FORWARD

Programming commands

BRAIN BOX

Coders can use **command blocks** to write instructions for a computer. Coders begin with the step they want the computer to do first. The next step goes below the first. Coders continue writing steps until there is a complete list of directions for the computer to follow.

Loopy Loops!

Write a program to help the cat catch the mouse.
Can you do it using only three commands?

Here are the commands you can use:

GO FORWARD 1

TURN RIGHT

LOOP [GO FORWARD 1] ____ TIMES

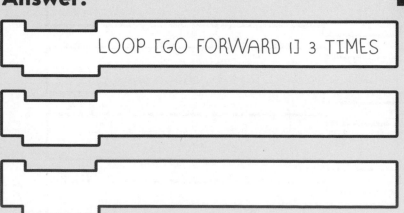

START

FINISH

Answer:

LOOP [GO FORWARD 1] 3 TIMES

A programmer's code can help the dog get to the bone, but three of the command blocks in the code below are NOT correct.

Circle the mistakes, then write the correct steps.

TURN RIGHT

LOOP [GO 1] 4 TIMES

TURN LEFT

LOOP [GO 1] 2 TIMES

TURN LEFT

LOOP [GO 1] 3 TIMES

TURN RIGHT

GO FORWARD 1

TURN RIGHT

GO FORWARD 1

TURN RIGHT

Which Bridge Is Best?

Three friends made bridges using cards, cups, and books. They want to build a bridge that supports at least one penny. They also want to predict, or guess, which bridge will hold the most pennies before it falls down.

Draw a circle around the bridge you think will hold the most pennies.

Draw a square around the bridge you think will hold the fewest pennies.

Anton

Himari

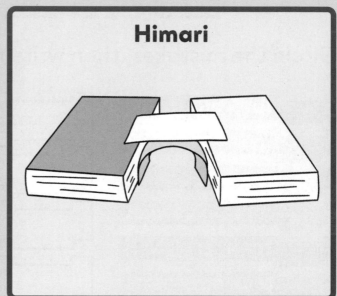

Sybil

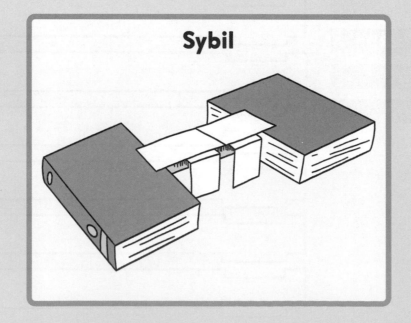

This graph shows how many coins each bridge could hold.

Read the graph and answer the questions.

Anton = 10 coins

Himari

Sybil

Did all the bridges support at least one coin? _____

How many coins did each bridge hold?

Anton	Himari	Sybil

Whose bridge held the most coins?

_____

Whose bridge held the fewest coins?

_____

Super Spy!

Before passwords, people used secret messages to keep their information private.

In this code, each letter of the alphabet has a number. What does the message say?

A	B	C	D	E	F	G	H	I	J
1	2	3	4	5	6	7	8	9	10

K	L	M	N	O	P	Q	R	S	T
11	12	13	14	15	16	17	18	19	20

U	V	W	X	Y	Z
21	22	23	24	25	26

BRAIN BOX

Secret messages are a kind of **encryption**. Encryption is one way that computers keep your information private. Encrypting words or messages changes the text into a form that only a person with the password can read.

___ ___ ___   ___ ___ ___   ___ ___!
25 15 21   4   9   4   9   20

Can you write your name in code?

YOUR NAME IN LETTERS:

YOUR NAME IN CODE (numbers):

ANSWER KEY

Some problems have only one answer. Some problems have many answers. Turn the page to check your work.

For additional resources, visit www.BrainQuest.com/grade2

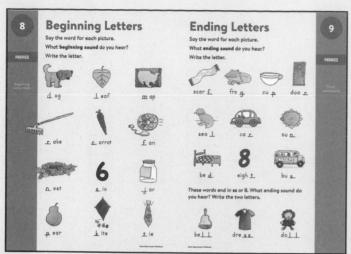

Beginning Letters

Say the word for each picture.
What **beginning sound** do you hear?
Write the letter.

d og   l eaf   m ap

r oke   c arrot   f an

n est   s ix   j ar

p ear   k ite   t ie

Ending Letters

Say the word for each picture.
What **ending sound** do you hear?
Write the letter.

scar f   fro g   cu p   doo r

sea l   ca r   su n

be d   eigh t   bu s

These words end in **ss** or **ll**. What ending sound do you hear? Write the two letters.

be ll   dre ss   do ll

It Takes Two

Say the word for each picture.
What beginning sound do you hear?
Find the correct **blend** in the boxes. Write it on the line.

bl br cl cr dr fl fr gl gr pl pr sc sl sk sm st sw tr

p r esent   s l ippers   s p oon   br ead   s t ool   s m oke

g r apes   s t amp   t r uck   cr ab   bl ock   s c ale

s w ing   f l ower   d r um   f r og   p l ant   c l ock

t r ee   s k is   g l asses

BRAIN BOX

Blends are two consonants that go together. You can hear both letters in a blend.

Example: plate

The blend in this word is p-l. When you say plate, you can hear both the p and l sounds.

12

Shh! Sounds

Complete each word with a **digraph** from the boxes.
Draw a line from the word to its picture.

ch sh th wh

wh eel
s h ark
ben ch
too th
w h istle
fi sh
c h eese

BRAIN BOX

Digraphs are two letters that make one sound.

Example: thing

The digraph in this word is t-h. When you say thing, you don't hear the t and h sounds separately. You hear the new th sound.

It Takes Three

Say the word for each picture.
Complete each word with a **consonant cluster** from the boxes.

scr squ str spr thr

s t r awberry   t h r ee   s t r eet

s q u irrel   s c r ub   s p r inkler

s t r ong   t h r one   s p r ay

s q u are   s c r ew   t h r ead

Lost Letters

Complete each word with a **consonant cluster** from the boxes.
Draw a line from the word to its picture.

st nk mp lt nd

ba n k
qui l t
ha n d
la m p
toa s t
sku n k

BRAIN BOX

A consonant cluster is a group of two or three consonants that are next to each other in a word.

Example: land

The consonant cluster in this word is n-d.

(page 15)

Complete each word with a **consonant cluster** from the boxes.
Draw a line from the word to its picture.

rd rk sk nt

pa r k
te n t
fo r k
ma s k
bi r d
boa r d game

15

Kite and Circle

Look at the **c** words in the boxes below.
If the word has a **hard c** sound, like **kite**, write the word next to the kite.
If the word has a **soft c** sound, like **circle**, write the word next to the circle.

kite
come
count
care
card

come   cent
count   care
cellar   card
city   cereal

circle
cellar
city
cent
cereal

BRAIN BOX

The letter c has two sounds: a hard c sound, as in cat, and a soft c sound, as in cell.

Goose and Jacket

Look at the **g** words in the boxes below.
If the word has a **hard g** sound, like **goose**, write the word next to the goose.
If the word has a **soft g** sound, like **jacket**, write the word next to the jacket.

jacket
giraffe
genius
gem
giant

giraffe   goat
game   gem
give   giant
genius   grow

goose
game
give
goat
grow

BRAIN BOX

The letter g has two sounds: a hard g sound as in girl and a soft g sound as in giant.

Picture Cards

Complete each word with a **short vowel**.

short a words
c a t   m a n
h a m   a nt
m a d   b a t

short e words
d e sk   b e ll
sl e d   b e d
h e n   p e n

short i words
f i sh   w i g
f i ll   p i g
l i d   h i d

short o words
d o ll   h o p
r o ck   f o x
n o t   p o t

short u words
pl u m   m u d
c u p   b u s
s u n   f u n

20

Short Vowel Sort

Read the words in the colored boxes.
Write each word next to the picture that has the same **short vowel** sound.

hot map big got dad
box red hug miss let
must pet mom up ran
ten top rush him fix

short a words
hat
hat
map
dad
ran

short e words
red
let
pet
ten

short i words
miss
him
fix
big

short o words
got
box
mom
top

short u words
hug
must
up
rush

At the Bay with Raina

Underline the words that have a **long a** sound.

Raina is heading to the bay with her family.

Before she leaves, she puts her hair in a braid.

It was raining yesterday, but the sun is shining brightly today.

Write **ai** or **ay** to complete the **long a** words and finish the story.

At the bay, Raina and her brother spr a y on sunblock to protect their skin.

Raina enjoys watching the bay's wildlife, like dolphins and r a y s.

The sky has turned gr a y, and it is time to go home.

Raina decides to p ai nt a picture of her special day.

BRAIN BOX

These letter combinations can make a long a sound: ai as in rain, and ay as in ray.

What Do You See?

Write **e**, **ea**, **ee**, or **ey** to complete the **long e** words.

My dad is driving us to the b ea ch.

There are thr ee of us in the car.

On the way, w e pass a tr ee.

There are lots of b ee s in the tr ee.

They are making hon ey.

Luckily, the bees don't sting m e!

Finally, we reach the s ea!

BRAIN BOX

These letter combinations can make a long e sound: e as in me, ea as in flea, ee as in tree, and ey as in money.

Sometimes, the letter e all by itself can also make a long e sound, as in he.

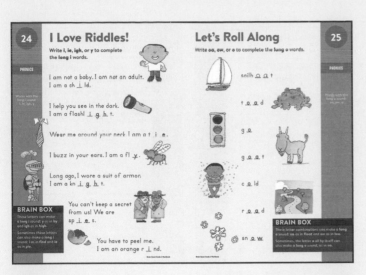

24 — I Love Riddles!

Write **i**, **ie**, **igh**, or **y** to complete the long **i** words.

I am not a baby. I am not an adult.
I am a ch **i** ld.

I help you see in the dark.
I am a flashl **igh** t.

Wear me around your neck. I am a t **ie** .

I buzz in your ears. I am a fl **y** .

Long ago, I wore a suit of armor.
I am a kn **igh** t.

You can't keep a secret from us! We are sp **ie** s.

You have to peel me.
I am an orange r **i** nd.

BRAIN BOX
These letters can make a long i sound: y as in by and igh as in high.
Sometimes these letters can also make a long i sound: i as in find and ie as in pie.

25 — Let's Roll Along

Write **oa**, **ow**, or **o** to complete the long **o** words.

snail b **oa** t

t **oa** d

g **o**

g **oa** t

c **o** ld

r **oa** d

sn **ow**

BRAIN BOX
These letter combinations can make a long o sound: oa as in float and ow as in low.
Sometimes, the letter o all by itself can also make a long o sound, as in no.

26 — A Few Clues

Write **u**, **ew**, **ue**, or **ui** to complete the words with the **oo** sound.

I am the color of the sky.
I am bl **ue** .

I can be an apple, an orange, or a grape.
I am fr **ui** t.

You can swim in me.
I am a p **oo** l.

The candle was still burning.
The man bl **ew** it out.

I stick things together.
I am gl **ue** .

I am a toy that's still in the box.
I am brand-n **ew** .

BRAIN BOX
These letter combinations make the /oo/ sound: ue as in due, ui as in juice, ew as in stool, and ew as in flew.

27 — Vote for E!

Add an **e** to the end of these **short vowel** words to make new **long vowel** words.

can   can **e**

man   man **e**

cap   cap **e**

cub   cub **e**

tub   tub **e**

pin   pin **e**

BRAIN BOX
A short vowel can become a long vowel when you add an e to the end of some words.
Example: kit + e = kite. When you add an e to the end of kit, you get kite. Kite has a long i sound.

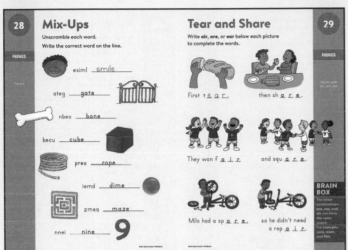

28 — Mix-Ups

Unscramble each word.
Write the correct word on the line.

esiml   **smile**

ateg   **gate**

nbeo   **bone**

becu   **cube**

preo   **rope**

iemd   **dime**

zmea   **maze**

nnei   **nine**

29 — Tear and Share

Write **air**, **are**, or **ear** below each picture to complete the words.

First t **ear** .   then sh **are** .

They won f **air** .   and squ **are** .

Milo had a sp **are** .   so he didn't need a rep **air** .

BRAIN BOX
The letter combinations are, ear, and air have different spellings but have the same sound.
For example, care, wear, and fair.

30 — Girl with Curls

Write **er**, **ir**, or **ur** to complete the words.

c **ur** tain

g **ir** l

c **ur** ls

sh **ir** t

f **er** n

wat **er**

sk **ir** t

BRAIN BOX
The letter combinations er, ir, and ur can all have the same sound. For example, fern, bird, and father.

31 — Clark's Chores

Write **ar**, **or**, **ore**, or **our** to complete the words.

Cl **ar** k lives on a f **ar** m.

Today, he has ch **ore** s to do.

First, Cl **ar** k feeds the h **or** se.

He puts hay in the b **ar** n.

He sweeps the p **or** ch.

He p **our** s milk for the cat.

Then, Cl **ar** k waters the vegetable g **ar** den.

He makes a list of things he needs from the st **ore** .

He picks f **our** ears of c **or** n for dinner.

BRAIN BOX
When an r follows a vowel, it slightly changes the vowel sound. Say the words out loud to hear the sounds in words with ar, or, ore, and our.

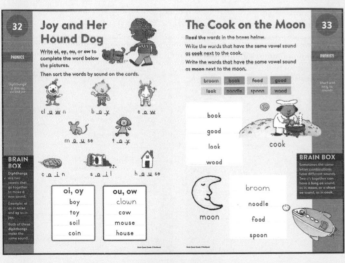

32 — Joy and Her Hound Dog

Write **oi**, **oy**, **ou**, or **ow** to complete the word below the pictures.
Then sort the words by sound on the cards.

cl **ow** n   b **oy**   c **ow**

m **ou** se   t **oy**

c **oi** n   s **oi** l   h **ou** se

oi, oy	ou, ow
boy	clown
toy	cow
soil	mouse
coin	house

BRAIN BOX
Diphthongs are two vowels that go together to make a new sound.
Example: oi as in noise and oy as in joy.
Both of these diphthongs make the same sound.

33 — The Cook on the Moon

Read the words in the boxes below.
Write the words that have the same vowel sound as **cook** next to the cook.
Write the words that have the same vowel sound as **moon** next to the moon.

broom   book   food   good
look   noodle spoon   wood

book
good
look
wood
cook

broom
noodle
food
spoon
moon

BRAIN BOX
Sometimes the same letter combinations have different sounds. Two o's together can have a long oo sound, as in moon, or a short oo sound, as in cook.

34 — Rhyme Time!

Write **al**, **all**, **aw**, or **o** to complete each rhyme.

b **all** on the w **all**

w **al** k and t **al** k

m **o** th in the br **o** th

str **aw** on a sees **aw**

l **o** ng s **o** ng

cr **aw** l and b **aw** l

BRAIN BOX
Various vowel combinations have the same sound: al, all, aw, o.

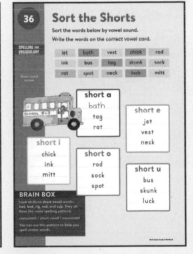

36 — Sort the Shorts

Sort the words below by vowel sound.
Write the words on the correct vowel card.

jet   bath   vest   chick   rod
ink   bus   tag   skunk   sock
rat   spot   neck   luck   mitt

short a
bath
tag
rat

short e
jet
vest
neck

short i
chick
ink
mitt

short o
rod
sock
spot

short u
bus
skunk
luck

BRAIN BOX
Look at these short vowel words: hat, bed, rig, rod, and cup. They all have the same spelling pattern: consonant / short vowel / consonant. You can use this pattern to help you spell similar words.

37

Answer the riddles with words from the boxes.

A pen is filled with me. I help you write.
I am **i** n **k** .

I am a baby bird. I am a **c** h **i** c **k** .

I fly high in the sky. I am a **j** e **t** .

I am yellow and take you to school.
I am a **b** u **s** .

I am black and white and very smelly.
I am a **s** k **u** n **k** .

You use me to fish. I am a fishing **r** o **d** .

I keep your foot warm and clean.
I am a **s** o **c** k .

You look at me when you want to know the price.
I am a price **t** a **g** .

You take me when you get dirty.
I am a **b** a **t** h .

38 — Crossword Craze

Complete the **long vowel** words with a vowel and a **final e**.
Write the words in the puzzle.

Across
2. She **a** t **e** the apple.
4. We have a flat t **i** r **e** .
5. A tree with needles: p **i** n **e** .
6. Our whole family gets together on New Year's **e** v **e** .
8. Four plus five equals n **i** n **e** .
9. A raisin is a dried g **r** a **p** e .

Down
1. A 3-D map of the world is a gl **o** b **e** .
3. Those are hers; th **e** s **e** are mine.
4. Another word for "melody": t **u** n **e** .
7. Tomatoes grow on a v **i** n **e** .
9. They g **a** v **e** the money they collected to charity.
10. Every Sunday I talk to my grandma on the ph **o** n **e** .

39

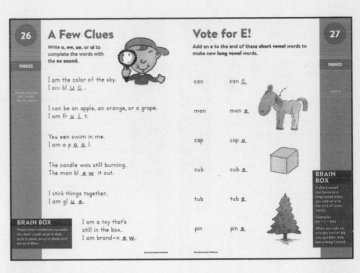

(Crossword grid)
g l o b e
a t e
h   g r a p e
t i r e   h
u   s   o
s v e n
p i n e   i
e   n i n e
       e

40 — Long a Words

Complete each sentence with a **long a** word from the boxes below.

okay   cake   paint
cage   play   mail

Artists like to draw and **paint** .

The bird is in the **cage** .

My favorite thing to eat is **cake** .

The postal worker delivered our **mail** .

We rehearsed our parts for the **play** .

He fell down, but he is **okay** .

Now sort the **long a** words on the cards below.

a_e
cage
cake

ai
paint
mail

ay
play
okay

BRAIN BOX
Look for these spelling patterns in long a words: a_e as in take, ay as in say, and ai as in paid.

Long e Words — 41

Complete each sentence with a **long e** word from the boxes below.

sheep | seal | money | dreams
me | Joey | sleep | be

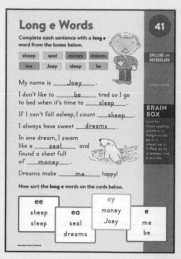

My name is __Joey__.

I don't like to __be__ tired so I go to bed when it's time to __sleep__.

If I can't fall asleep, I count __sheep__.

I always have sweet __dreams__.

In one dream, I swam like a __seal__ and found a chest full of __money__.

Dreams make __me__ happy!

Now sort the **long e** words on the cards below.

ee — sheep, sleep
ea — seal, dreams
ey — money, Joey
e — me, be

Long i Words — 42

Complete each sentence with a **long i** word from the boxes below.

pie | sky | ice | high
bright | tide | rice | twice

Some birds can fly very __high__.

When water freezes, it becomes __ice__.

The opposite of dark is __bright__.

In cooking class, she baked an apple __pie__.

If you checked your work two times, it's done __twice__.

The clouds drifted across the __sky__.

My favorite dish is beans and __rice__.

We saw the crabs at low __tide__.

Now sort the **long i** words on the cards below.

i_e — ice, twice, rice, tide
y — sky
igh — high, bright
ie — pie

Long o Words — 43

Complete each sentence with a **long o** word from the boxes below.

toast | wrote | rainbow | grow
throat | go | gold | note

At the end of the __rainbow__ there is a pot of __gold__.

I __wrote__ a letter to a friend at camp.

I eat __toast__ with butter for breakfast.

My mom always puts a __note__ in my lunch box.

The opposite of stop is __go__.

I'm sick. I have a sore __throat__.

Every day I __grow__ bigger.

Now sort the **long o** words on the cards below.

oa — throat, toast
ow — rainbow, grow
o — gold, go
o_e — wrote, note

Long u Words — 44

Complete each sentence with a **long u** word from the boxes below.

unicorn | use | utensils | music
argue | huge | mule | cute

A __unicorn__ has a horn on its head.

I __use__ colored pencils in art class.

When my sister and I disagree, we __argue__.

Puppies and kittens are so __cute__!

The opposite of tiny is __huge__.

A knife and a fork are eating __utensils__.

The __mule__ carried the heavy bags up the mountain.

I listen to pop __music__.

Now sort the **long u** words on the cards below.

ue — argue
u_e — use, cute, huge, mule
u — unicorn, utensils, music

Silent Letters — 45

These words all have **silent letters**. Say each word out loud as you copy it. Then circle the silent letter.

comb — com(b)
lamb — lam(b)
sign — sig(n)
knife — (k)nife
kneel — (k)neel
sword — s(w)ord
high — hig(h)
write — (w)rite
sigh — sig(h)

Write a sentence using one of the words above.

_____
_____

Compound It! — 46

Use a word from the boxes below to make a compound word. Use the pictures as clues.

plane | berry | book | robe
fish | pot | hole | cake

pan + __cake__ = __pancake__
air + __plane__ = __airplane__
both + __robe__ = __bathrobe__
straw + __berry__ = __strawberry__
key + __hole__ = __keyhole__
note + __book__ = __notebook__
flower + __pot__ = __flowerpot__
gold + __fish__ = __goldfish__

47

Draw a line from a word in the green column to a word in the blue column to make a common **compound word**. Then write the compound word in the orange column.

back	cage	backbone
camp	bone	campfire
bag	pole	bagpipes
book	work	bookcase
grape	flakes	grapevine
sky	line	skyline
home	pipes	homework
bean	fire	beanpole
bird	case	birdcage
snow	vine	snowflakes

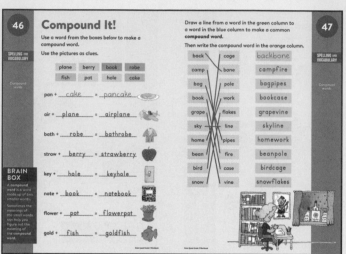

The Why of Y — 48

The words below all end in y, but they are not all pronounced the same way. Sort the words by vowel sound.

Write the y words with the same sound as **spy** on the spy card.

Write the y words with the same sound as **bunny** on the bunny card.

baby | cry | happy | my
story | fly | mommy | lullaby | sky

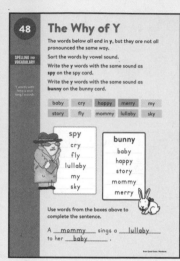

spy — cry, fly, lullaby, my, sky

bunny — baby, happy, story, mommy, merry

Use words from the boxes above to complete the sentence.

A __mommy__ sings a __lullaby__ to her __baby__.

A Silly Story — 49

Read the story. Circle all the words that end in y. Then sort the words on the cards below.

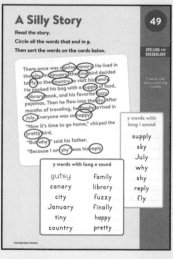

There once was a (gutsy) (canary). He lived in the (city). In (January) the (tiny) bird decided to (fly) to the (country) to visit his (family). He packed his bag with a (supply) of food, a (library) book, and his favorite (fuzzy) pajamas. Then he flew into the (sky). After months of traveling, he (finally) arrived in (July). Everyone was so (happy).

"Now it's time to go home," chirped the (pretty) bird.

"But (why)?" said his father.

"Because I am (shy)," was his (reply).

y words with long i sound — supply, sky, July, why, shy, reply, fly

y words with long e sound — gutsy, canary, city, January, tiny, country, family, library, fuzzy, finally, happy, pretty

Zane's Yard Sale — 50

Complete the words that have the same vowel sound as **yard**.

al__a r__m clock
j__a r__ of m__a r__bles
toy c__a r__s
y__a r__n
toy f__a r__m
shin gu__a r__ds
st__a r__ sweater

Spell Like a Shark! — 51

Write all the **ar** words from the boxes below in alphabetical order.

start | party | cart | garden
art | march | park | large
far | hard | harm | bar

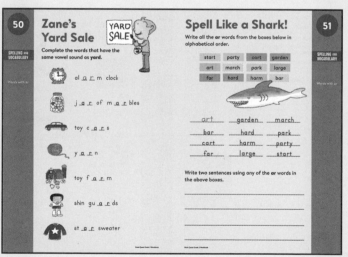

__art__ __garden__ __march__
__bar__ __hard__ __park__
__cart__ __harm__ __party__
__far__ __large__ __start__

Write two sentences using any of the **ar** words in the above boxes.

_____
_____
_____
_____

All About Fern — 52

Circle all the words that have the same vowel sound as **Fern**.

My name is (Fern) and I am the (third) tallest (girl) in my class. I am also the only (person) in my class who has (curly) hair. Can you believe that?

This is my favorite book. I got it for my (birthday). I am (learning) all about Florence Nightingale, the famous (nurse). When I grow up, I want to be a (nurse) too.

Say each word you circled. Listen to the vowel sound. Sort the words by spelling pattern on the **ear, er, ir, ur** cards below.

ir — third, girl, birthday
er — Fern, person
ur — curly, nurse
ear — learning

Spell Like a Bird — 53

Say each word in the colored boxes. Sort the words by spelling pattern on the cards below.

pearl | lantern | burn | search
bird | curb | lavender | first
hurt | shirt | letter | earth
purpose | chirp | perfect | glitter
urgent | early | dirty | earn

ur — urgent, burn, purpose, hurt, curb
ear — search, earth, pearl, earn, early
ir — first, bird, chirp, dirty, shirt
er — lavender, letter, glitter, lantern, perfect

A Cow in the House! — 54

Complete the clues with words that make the /ow/ sound. Write the words in the puzzle.

Across
1. Milk comes from c__o w s__.
3. A h__o u s e__ is a building where you live.
5. Is your hair the color br__o w n__?
7. What goes up must come d__o w n__.
9. A circus cl__o w n__ makes people laugh.
11. I use a t__o w e l__ to get dry.

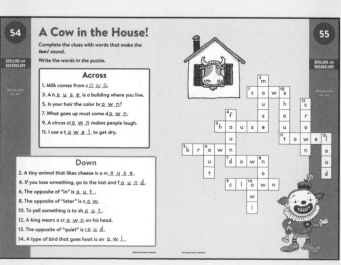

Down
2. A tiny animal that likes cheese is a m__o u s e__.
4. If you lose something, go to the lost and f__o u n d__.
6. The opposite of "in" is __o u t__.
8. The opposite of "later" is n__o w__.
10. To yell something is to sh__o u t__.
12. A king wears a cr__o w n__ on his head.
13. The opposite of "quiet" is l__o u d__.
14. A type of bird that goes hoot is an __o w l__.

Roy Points — 56

Sort the words by spelling pattern on the cards below.

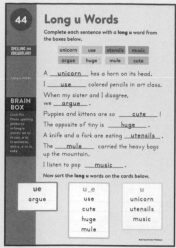

coin | boy | toy
voice | oyster | noise
join | oil | boil | royal | point
loyal | enjoy | choice | annoy | destroy

oi — coin, oil, voice, boil, noise, point, join, choice

oy — boy, enjoy, toy, loyal, oyster, annoy, royal, destroy

Moose and Books — 57

All the words in the boxes are oo words, but they are not all pronounced the same way.

Write the oo words with the same sound as **moose** on the moose card.

Write the oo words with the same sound as **book** on the book card.

balloon · hood · spoon · wood · foot
tooth · look · shook · spooky · loose

book
look
hood
wood
foot
shook

moose
balloon
spooky
spoon
tooth
loose

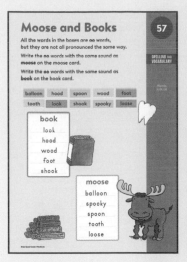

Opposites! — 58

Read each sentence. Circle the **antonym** of the underlined word in the sentence.

A great dane is a <u>large</u> dog!
(small) giant big

The balloon flew up in the air.
high (down) left

She went to the <u>front</u> of the line.
top start (back)

It is so <u>hot</u> today!
warm (cold) rainy

Draw a line from each word to its **antonym**.

terrible — dry
before — thrilled
disappointed — after
soaked — fabulous

BRAIN BOX
Antonyms are words that have opposite meanings. Happy and sad are antonyms.

So Many Snowflakes! — 59

Draw a line from each snowflake to its synonym.

correct — say
little — terrific
smart — wise
great — right
gone — too
also — small
speak — left

Fill in the blanks with **synonyms** from the boxes below.

challenging · sparkle · moist · missing

lost ___missing___   difficult ___challenging___
shine ___sparkle___   damp ___moist___

Write It Right — 60

Circle the correct **homophone** in each sentence.

It is half past the our /(hour).
There is a pair /(pear) tree in the yard.
She broke her (right)/ write leg.
The clouds are hiding the son /(sun).

On the lines below, write two sentences for two of the words you did not circle.

_____
_____
_____
_____

BRAIN BOX
Homophones are words that sound the same but have different spellings and meanings. Eight and ate are homophones.

Same Sounds — 61

I am going to ballet class (too)/ two.
Look at that fish's I /(eye)!
All the boats are on (sale)/ sail.
The movie is playing for two weaks /(weeks) only.

On the lines below, write two sentences for two of the words you did not circle.

_____
_____
_____
_____

More than One — 62

Write the plural for each word by adding **s** or **es**.

apple ___apples___
ax ___axes___
glass ___glasses___
box ___boxes___
cat ___cats___
sandwich ___sandwiches___
fox ___foxes___
pen ___pens___
brush ___brushes___
crutch ___crutches___
watch ___watches___
bus ___buses___

BRAIN BOX
Plural means more than one.
Add s to make most nouns plural.
Add es if the noun ends in sh, ch, tch, s, or x.

Irregular Plural — 63

Each box shows a picture of a word that is irregular when plural. Circle the correct irregular plural. Then rewrite the correct answer on the line below it.

wemen / (women) / womenes
___women___

foots / footes / (feet)
___feet___

(dice) / dies / dices
___dice___

mouse / (mice) / mouzes
___mice___

childs / (children) / children
___children___

tooth / tonths / (teeth)
___teeth___

BRAIN BOX
Some plurals are irregular. This means you don't add s or es at the end to make the word plural. You have to change the whole word.

Tell Me About It! — 66

Read each group of words. Underline the **statements**.

<u>I like to go to the ice cream store.</u>
The pictures on the window.
<u>My mother, my sister, and I.</u>
<u>We eat our favorite flavors.</u>
The chocolate ice cream.
<u>My mom likes vanilla.</u>
The books resting by our feet.
<u>I sit on the bench.</u>
<u>I have red shoes.</u>

BRAIN BOX
A sentence is a group of words that express a complete thought.
All sentences begin with a capital letter.
A statement is a sentence that explains or tells what someone or something does. End a statement with a period.

67

Write each statement correctly. Begin with a capital letter and end with a period.

the swimming class begins at noon
___The swimming class begins at noon.___
i can dive off the high board
___I can dive off the high board.___
sara does a backflip
___Sara does a backflip.___
the little kids wear water wings
___The little kids wear water wings.___
our lifeguard's name is Rena
___Our lifeguard's name is Rena.___

Say What? — 68

Rewrite each sentence.
If the sentence asks a **question**, add a question mark.
If the sentence is a **statement**, add a period.

is it raining hard
___Is it raining hard?___
sam likes his green boots
___Sam likes his green boots.___
can we jump in the puddles
___Can we jump in the puddles?___
will you play with me after school
___Will you play with me after school?___
i hope it stops raining
___I hope it stops raining.___
what did the forecast say
___What did the forecast say?___
do you see a rainbow
___Do you see a rainbow?___

BRAIN BOX
A question is a sentence that asks something. End a question with a question mark. Remember to begin all sentences with a capital letter.

The Race Begins! — 69

Rewrite each sentence as an **exclamation**.

look how fast I can run
___Look how fast I can run!___
tie your shoelaces
___Tie your shoelaces!___
we love racing
___We love racing!___
on your mark, get set, go
___On your mark, get set, go!___
hurry to the finish line
___Hurry to the finish line!___

Oh no! Jamal is still reading when he should be going to sleep.
Write two **commands** that his father might say to him.

BRAIN BOX
An exclamation is a sentence that tells about strong feelings, such as surprise, excitement, or fear. End an exclamation with an exclamation point.
A statement is a sentence that tells someone to do something. End a command with either a period or an exclamation point.

A Picture Tells a Story — 70

Write each sentence correctly. Then circle the type of sentence it is.

is the skateboard in the closet
___Is the skateboard in the closet?___
statement · (question) · exclamation · command

wear a hat and a sweater
___Wear a hat and a sweater.___
statement · question · exclamation · (command)

i think we should go to the park
___I think we should go to the park.___
(statement) · question · exclamation · command

watch out for the ghost
___Watch out for the ghost!___
statement · question · (exclamation) · command

Sentence Scramble — 71

First, unscramble the words to write a **statement**. Then use the same words to write a **question**. Remember to **capitalize** and use correct **punctuation**.

come · party · they · will · to · the
___They will come to the party.___
___Will they come to the party?___

sleep · can · on · bed · dog · my · the
___The dog can sleep on my bed. Can the dog sleep on my bed?___

he · get · mail · should · the
___He should get the mail. Should he get the mail?___

cookie · can · jar · open · the
___I can open the cookie jar. Can I open the cookie jar?___

People, Places, and Things — 72

Underline the **nouns** in each sentence.

The <u>students</u> borrowed <u>books</u> from the <u>library</u>.
The <u>baker</u> sold <u>bread</u> at the <u>market</u>.
The <u>teacher</u> brought his <u>guitar</u> to <u>school</u>.
The <u>children</u> sat on the <u>grass</u> in the <u>park</u>.
The <u>president</u> of the <u>country</u> made a <u>speech</u>.
The <u>captain</u> sailed her <u>ship</u> down the <u>river</u>.
The <u>farmer</u> grew <u>corn</u> on their <u>farm</u>.
My <u>sister</u> is the top <u>speller</u> in our <u>state</u>.

73

The <u>waiter</u> wears a <u>uniform</u> to the <u>restaurant</u>.
The <u>pilot</u> landed the <u>plane</u> at the <u>airport</u>.

Now sort all the **nouns** you underlined on the cards.

people
students
baker
teacher
children
president
captain
farmer
sister
waiter
pilot

places
library
market
school
park
country
river
farm
state
restaurant
airport

things
books
bread
guitar
grass
speech
ship
corn
speller
uniform
plane

BRAIN BOX
A noun is a part of speech that names a person, place, thing, or idea. Parents, camp, computer, and happiness are all nouns.

And Away We Go!

Underline the proper nouns in each sentence.

Proper nouns

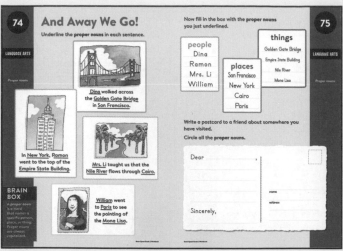

Dina walked across the **Golden Gate Bridge** in **San Francisco**.

In **New York**, **Ramon** went to the top of the **Empire State Building**.

Mrs. Li taught us that the **Nile River** flows through **Cairo**.

William went to **Paris** to see the painting of the **Mona Lisa**.

BRAIN BOX
A proper noun is a word that names a specific person, place, or thing. Proper nouns are always capitalized.

Now fill in the box with the **proper nouns** you just underlined.

Proper nouns

people	places	things
Dina	San Francisco	Golden Gate Bridge
Ramon	New York	Empire State Building
Mrs. Li	Cairo	Nile River
William	Paris	Mona Lisa

Write a postcard to a friend about somewhere you have visited.
Circle all the proper nouns.

Dear _____

_____
_____

Sincerely,

name
address

Fun at the Playground!

The words in the circles are all **pronouns**.

She   We   It   He   They

Pronouns

Rewrite each sentence using the pronoun that can take the place of the underlined word(s) in each sentence.

Max and Lila are on the seesaw.
They are on the seesaw.

Juan swings through the air.
He swings through the air.

Amy zooms down the slide.
She zooms down the slide.

All of us are having a good time.
We are having a good time.

The playground is busy.
It is busy.

BRAIN BOX
A pronoun is a word that can take the place of a noun.

Dog Day

Underline the **subject** of each sentence.
Circle the **noun**.

Subjects

The (park) is a busy place.

(Ollie) walks his dogs there every afternoon.

The biggest (dog) is named Hamlet.

Ollie's favorite is a (poodle) named Fifi.

The (pets) run and play together.

Some (dogs) bark at the squirrels.

The (squirrels) stay in the trees.

BRAIN BOX
The subject tells who or what a sentence is about.
The subject always has a noun or pronoun in it.

Batter Up!

Choose a word from a baseball to complete each sentence.

swings   holds   hits   steps   picks   throws

The batter _picks_ up the bat.

She _steps_ up to home plate.

The catcher _holds_ up her mitt.

The pitcher _throws_ the ball.

The batter _swings_.

She _hits_ the ball.

Write a sentence describing your favorite sport.
Underline the verb in your sentence.

_____
_____
_____

Bake a Cake!

Underline the **verb** in each sentence.

Malik <u>mixes</u> the cake batter in a bowl.

Carla <u>pours</u> the batter into a pan.

Dad <u>puts</u> the pan in the oven.

Ding! Dad <u>takes</u> the cake out of the oven.

Write two sentences about what Carla and Malik will do next.
Underline the verbs in your sentences.

_____
_____
_____

BRAIN BOX
A verb is an action word. It tells what someone or something does.

Visit the Farm!

Change the underlined **verb** so that the action happened in the past.

Present- and past-tense verbs

Malik and Carla <u>visit</u> a local farm.
Yesterday, Malik and Carla <u>visited</u> a local farm.

Carla <u>likes</u> to feed the chickens.
Carla <u>liked</u> to feed the chickens.

Malik <u>looks</u> for the goat.
Malik <u>looked</u> for the goat.

Carla <u>opens</u> the door to the barn.
Carla <u>opened</u> the door to the barn.

Malik <u>walks</u> the horse inside.
Malik <u>walked</u> the horse inside.

Carla and Malik <u>enjoy</u> their time at the farm.
Carla and Malik <u>enjoyed</u> their time at the farm.

Time to Paint

These sentences are written in present tense, then past tense.
Fill in the blanks with the past- or present-tense form of **to have**.

Irregular verbs: to have

I **have** paints. I _had_ paints.

He **has** brushes. He _had_ brushes.

We _have_ fun. We **had** fun.

They **have** canvases. They _had_ canvases.

Now use the correct form of the verb **to have** to answer these questions.

What color eyes do you have?
I _____

What favorite toy did you have as a baby?
I _____

BRAIN BOX
The verb **to have** is irregular. This means it doesn't follow the same rules as most regular verbs.

to have	
present tense	past tense
I have	I had
You have	You had
He / She / It has	He / She / It had
We / They have	We / They had

Time for a Picnic!

Fill in the correct form of the verb **to be** to complete each sentence.
Circle **present** if the verb tells about the **present**.
Circle **past** if the verb tells about the **past**.

Irregular verbs: to be

The picnic _was_ last Sunday.
present   (past)

Today it _is_ raining.
(present)   past

Luckily, the weather _was_ dry last week.
present   (past)

We _were_ in the park until it got dark.
present   (past)

I _was_ tired when I got home from the picnic.
present   (past)

I _am_ glad to be inside now.
(present)   past

BRAIN BOX
The verb **to be** is irregular. This means it doesn't follow the same rules as most regular verbs.

to be	
present tense	past tense
I am	I was
You are	You were
He / She / It is	He / She / It was
We / They are	We / They were

To Have and to Be

Use a form of **to have** or **to be** to answer each question.

Irregular verbs: to be, to have

What is the weather like today?
_____

What was the weather like yesterday?
_____

Do you have an umbrella today?
_____

Draw a picture of you and a friend in the picture frame.
Then answer the questions below.

I _am_ _8_ years old.

My best friend _is_ ____ years old.

This year, we _are_ in the ____ grade.

Last year, we _were_ in the ____ grade.

Who Did What?

Use the drawings to help you match the **subjects** to the **predicates**.

Draw a line from the words in the SUBJECT column to the matching words in the PREDICATE column.

SUBJECT	PREDICATE
The family	pointed the sign.
Lia	squeezed each lemon.
Ken	sold the lemonade.
Their parents	cut the lemons in half.

Write sentences using the subjects and predicates you matched. Circle the noun(s) in the **subject**.
Underline the verb in the **predicate**.

The (family) <u>sold</u> the lemonade.

(Lia) <u>squeezed</u> each lemon.

(Ken) <u>painted</u> the sign.

Their (parents) <u>cut</u> the lemons in half.

BRAIN BOX
The naming part of a sentence is called the subject. It tells who or what the sentence is about.
The telling part of a sentence is called the predicate. It tells what the subject does.

Subjects and predicates

Day at the Carnival

Look at each picture and read the caption.
Circle the **noun**.
Underline the **adjective**.

Adjectives

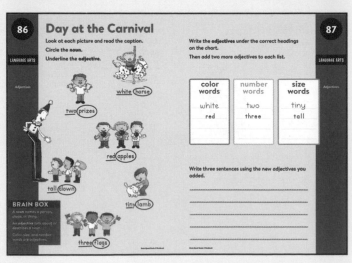

<u>white</u> (horse)

<u>two</u> (prizes)

<u>red</u> (apples)

<u>tall</u> (clown)

<u>tiny</u> (lamb)

<u>three</u> (flags)

BRAIN BOX
A noun names a person, place, or thing.
An adjective tells about or describes a noun.
Color, size, and number words are adjectives.

Write the **adjectives** under the correct headings on the chart.
Then add two more adjectives to each list.

Adjectives

color words	number words	size words
white	two	tiny
red	three	tall

Write three sentences using the new adjectives you added.

_____
_____
_____

Five Senses

Circle the **noun** in each caption.
Underline the **adjective**.

Sensory adjectives

<u>salty</u> (popcorn)   <u>loud</u> (noise)

<u>stinky</u> (cheese)   <u>wet</u> (elephant)

<u>colorful</u> (balloons)   <u>delicious</u> (hot dog)

Write look, feel, taste, smell, or sound by the correct body parts below.

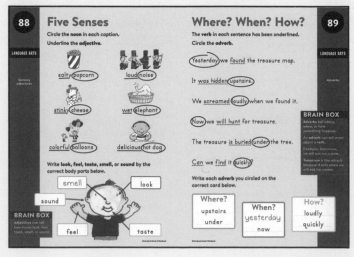

smell   look
sound
feel   taste

BRAIN BOX
Adjectives can tell how nouns look, feel, taste, smell, or sound.

Where? When? How?

The **verb** in each sentence has been underlined.
Circle the **adverb**.

Adverbs

(Yesterday) we <u>found</u> the treasure map.

It <u>was hidden</u> (upstairs).

We <u>screamed</u> (loudly) when we found it.

(Now) we <u>will hunt</u> for treasure.

The treasure <u>is buried</u> (under) the tree.

<u>Can</u> we <u>find</u> it (quickly)?

Write each adverb you circled on the correct card below.

Where?	When?	How?
upstairs	yesterday	loudly
under	now	quickly

BRAIN BOX
Adverbs tell where, when, or how something happens.
An adverb can tell more about a verb.
Example: Tomorrow, we will eat ice cream.
Tomorrow is the adverb because it tells when we will eat ice cream.

Bear Bakes

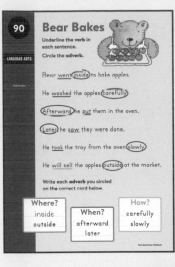

Underline the **verb** in each sentence.
Circle the **adverb**.

Bear <u>went</u> inside to bake apples.

He <u>washed</u> the apples (carefully).

(Afterward) he <u>put</u> them in the oven.

(Later) he <u>saw</u> they were done.

He <u>took</u> the tray from the oven (slowly).

He will <u>sell</u> the apples (outside) at the market.

Write each **adverb** you circled
on the correct card below.

Where?	When?	How?
inside	afterward	carefully
outside	later	slowly

"Bed in Summer" is a poem that rhymes.

Fill in the chart with **rhyming words** that end the lines of the poem. Then add your own rhyming word.

night	way	see
candlelight	day	tree

feet	you	play
street	blue	day

Now answer the questions.

How does the child in the poem feel?

_____

How do you feel in the summertime?

_____

"Yes!" said Wind. "We will have a contest!"
Sun looked down and saw an old man strolling by. He wore a hat and an overcoat.
"Do you see that old man?" Sun asked. "Whichever of us can make him take off his overcoat is the strongest. Wind, I will let you go first." Then Sun hid behind a cloud to watch.

Wind huffed. Wind puffed. Wind began to blow. The trees bowed down even lower. The windows in the farmhouse shook louder. Wind blew strong and cold.

The man said. "Brrr! What a cold, strong wind!" Then he buttoned up his overcoat. Wind blew stronger. Wind blew colder.

(continued on next page)

2

Who are the main characters in the story?

<u>The main characters are Wind, Sun,</u>

<u>and the old man.</u>

What challenge do Sun and Wind agree to?

<u>They want to make the old man take his</u>

<u>coat off.</u>

What happened when Wind blew?

<u>The old man buttoned his overcoat.</u>

_____

What happened when Sun shone?

<u>The old man took off his overcoat.</u>

_____

Who won the contest?

<u>Sun won the contest.</u>

What would happen if Rain came along and entered the contest?

_____

How does having a contest solve an argument?

_____

Why was there no time for the children to play?

<u>The children couldn't play because</u>

<u>they were always working.</u>

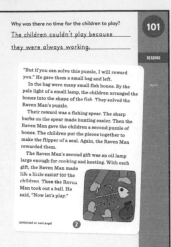

"But if you can solve this puzzle, I will reward you." He gave them a small bag and left.

In the bag were many small fish bones. By the pale light of a small lamp, the children arranged the bones into the shape of the fish. They solved the Raven Man's puzzle.

Their reward was a fishing spear. The sharp barbs on the spear made hunting easier. Then the Raven Man gave the children a second puzzle of bones. The children put the pieces together to make the flipper of a seal. Again, the Raven Man rewarded them.

The Raven Man's second gift was an oil lamp large enough for cooking and heating. With each gift, the Raven Man made life a little easier for the children. Then the Raven Man took out a ball. He said, "Now let's play."

(continued on next page)

2

Outside in the freezing darkness, the children and the Raven Man played catch. Suddenly the ball caught on the Raven Man's sharp beak. The ball ripped open. Through the tear, the sun escaped and lit the sky. For the first time, the world felt the warmth of sunshine.

And that is how day was created out of night.

THE END

3

What was inside the ball the children were playing with?

<u>The sun was in the ball.</u>

What two gifts did the Raven Man give the children?

<u>The Raven Man gave the children a</u>

<u>fishing spear and an oil lamp.</u>

How do you think the children feel at the end of the story? Why?

_____

How would this story ending be different if the visitor were a Rabbit Man instead of the Raven Man?

_____

What happened first, next, and last? Number the pictures to show the order.

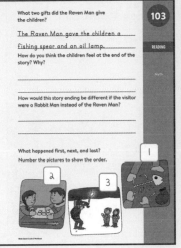

Plot the play you just read.
Tell what happens in the **beginning, middle,** and **end** of the play.

Beginning Why won't the old man let the young man rest under the tree?
<u>The old man tells the young man that</u>
<u>he owns the tree and its shade.</u>

Middle What does the young man do next?
<u>The young man buys the shade.</u>

_____

End How does the story end?
<u>Everyone enjoys the shade of the tree.</u>

Can you think of a different ending for the folktale? Write it here.

_____

Draw a line to match each **cause** and **effect**.

Causes | **Effects**

Causes	Effects
Lena learned it was going to rain.	They put their shin guards in their backpacks.
Grace and Justin play soccer on Monday.	They talk and joke together.
Lena, Grace, and Justin are friends.	She took an umbrella to school.

Write three other titles for this story.
Circle the one you like best.

_____
_____
_____

Who is who? Write the name of the character in the picture on the line below it.

<u>Freya</u>

<u>Athena</u>

<u>Athena</u>

<u>Freya</u>

Anansi took a thorn from his thorn tree and lowered himself into Elephant's garden. Clever Anansi picked the best melon. He used the thorn to make a hole in it. Then the hungry spider crawled inside.

Anansi ate and ate and ate, until he could eat no more. Finally, Anansi tried to crawl out of the hole. But he was stuck! He had eaten too much, and now the hole was too small. How would Anansi get out?

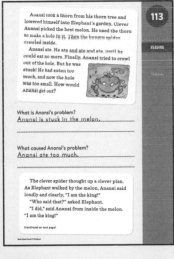

What is Anansi's problem?
<u>Anansi is stuck in the melon.</u>

What caused Anansi's problem?
<u>Anansi ate too much.</u>

The clever spider thought up a clever plan. As Elephant walked by the melon, Anansi said loudly and clearly, "I am the king!"
"Who said that?" asked Elephant.
"I did," said Anansi from inside the melon. "I am the king!"

(continued on next page)

Surprised, Elephant said, "You're a melon, not a king! But a talking melon is rare. I will take you to the king."

Elephant presented the melon to the king. The king said, "Why have you brought me a melon, Elephant? I have melons of my own."
"Not like this one, Your Majesty," said Elephant.
Then the melon said, "I am the king!"
"Who said that?" demanded the king angrily.

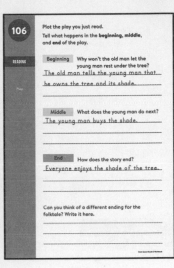

How does the king feel? Why does he feel that way?

<u>Answers may vary. Sample answer:</u>
<u>The king feels angry because the</u>
<u>melon is lying by saying it is the king.</u>

"I did," said the melon. "I am the king!"
"You are not the king! You are a melon!" roared the king. Then the king took the melon and threw it.

The melon sailed through the air all the way back to Elephant's garden. The melon landed SPLAT! and cracked wide open. Anansi jumped out and scurried up a coconut tree.

Elephant returned home. He said to his melons, "You are melons. Just melons! Not kings!"

From behind a coconut, Anansi said, "Melon kings! How silly!"

Elephant looked up into his coconut tree and cried, "Oh no! Talking coconuts!"

THE END

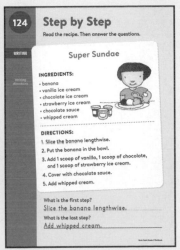

How did Anansi solve his problem?

<u>He tricked Elephant and the king</u>
<u>into helping him.</u>

Step by Step

Read the recipe. Then answer the questions.

Super Sundae

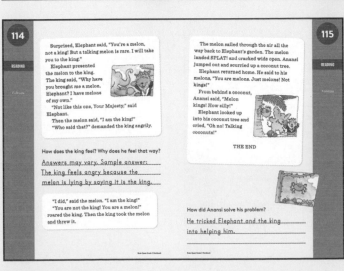

INGREDIENTS:
- banana
- vanilla ice cream
- chocolate ice cream
- strawberry ice cream
- chocolate sauce
- whipped cream

DIRECTIONS:
1. Slice the banana lengthwise.
2. Put the banana in the bowl.
3. Add 1 scoop of vanilla, 1 scoop of chocolate, and 1 scoop of strawberry ice cream.
4. Cover with chocolate sauce.
5. Add whipped cream.

What is the first step?
<u>Slice the banana lengthwise.</u>

What is the last step?
<u>Add whipped cream.</u>

---

160 — Bundles of Bugs

MATH SKILLS

Place value to tens

Look at the **numerals** and words on each jar.
Write the number they equal on the line.

1 ten + 7 ones = **17**

3 tens + 8 ones = **38**

7 tens + 0 ones = **70**

9 tens + 3 ones = **93**

BRAIN BOX

Place value tells us the value of each digit in a number. Look at 36:

tens	ones
3	6

The **3** tells us there are 3 tens.
The **6** tells us there are 6 ones.

161 — Hop to It!

MATH SKILLS

Place value to hundreds

Circle the correct **numeral**.

Circle the ones. 12**3**
Circle the tens. **4**5
Circle the hundreds. **8**36
Circle the tens. 5**1**7
Circle the hundreds. **3**82
Circle the ones. 69**7**

	hundreds	tens	ones
624	6	2	4
391	3	9	1
105	1	0	5
879	8	7	9
243	2	4	3

BRAIN BOX

A 3-digit number is made up of hundreds, tens, and ones. Look at 834:

hundreds	tens	ones
8	3	4

The **8** tells us there are 8 hundreds. The **3** tells us there are 3 tens. The **4** tells us there are 4 ones.

162 — Lucky Thousands

MATH SKILLS

Place value to thousands

Write the **place value** for each numeral on the chart.

	thousands	hundreds	tens	ones
1,843	1	8	4	3
2,692	2	6	9	2
7,034	7	0	3	4
4,880	4	8	8	0
9,718	9	7	1	8

Draw a line to match the words to the number.

8 thousands, 5 hundreds, 3 tens, 5 ones — 9,101
9 thousands, 1 hundred, 0 tens, 1 one — 6,464
6 thousands, 4 hundreds, 4 tens, 6 ones — 6,446
6 thousands, 4 hundreds, 6 tens, 4 ones — 8,535

BRAIN BOX

A 4-digit number is made up of thousands, hundreds, tens, and ones. Look at 4,627:

thousands	hundreds	tens	ones
4	6	2	7

The **4** tells us there are 4 thousands. The **6** tells us there are 6 hundreds. The **2** tells us there are 2 tens. The **7** tells us there are 7 ones.

163 — Words to Numbers

MATH SKILLS

Place value

Draw a line to match the number to the words.

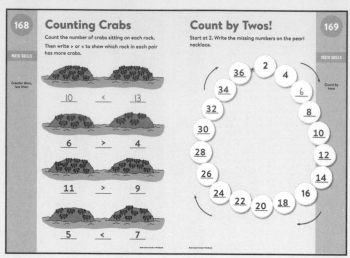

21 — 1 ten, 2 ones
1,586 — 3 hundreds, 1 ten
310 — 1 thousand, 5 hundreds, 8 tens, 6 ones
301 — 2 tens, 1 one
1,856 — 3 hundreds, 1 one
12 — 1 thousand, 8 hundreds, 5 tens, 6 ones

Write the value of each digit in **452** using words:

Four hundreds, five tens,

two ones

164 — Words to Numbers

MATH SKILLS

Write the numerals

Write the numbers on the apples.

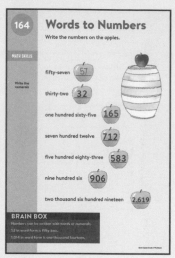

fifty-seven — **57**
thirty-two — **32**
one hundred sixty-five — **165**
seven hundred twelve — **712**
five hundred eighty-three — **583**
nine hundred six — **906**
two thousand six hundred nineteen — **2,619**

BRAIN BOX

Numbers can be written with words or numerals.
52 in word form is fifty-two.
1,014 in word form is one thousand fourteen.

167 — Compare the Candles

MATH SKILLS

Greater than, less than

Write the number of candles beneath each cake.
Then write > or < to show which cake has more.

12 < 13

4 < 9

10 > 7

5 < 8

11 > 8

BRAIN BOX

< means less than.
> means greater than.

Example: 4 < 6
This less than sign tells us that 4 is less than 6.

Example: 10 > 5
The greater than sign tells us that 10 is greater than 5.

168 — Counting Crabs

MATH SKILLS

Greater than, less than

Count the number of crabs sitting on each rock.
Then write > or < to show which rock in each pair has more crabs.

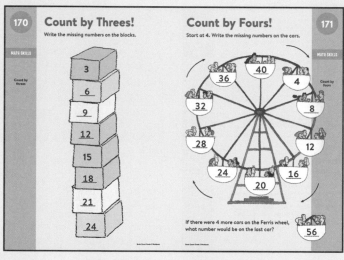

10 < 13

6 > 4

11 > 9

5 < 7

169 — Count by Twos!

MATH SKILLS

Count by twos

Start at 2. Write the missing numbers on the pearl necklace.

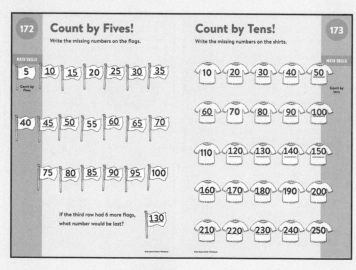

2, 4, 6, 8, 10, 12, 14, 16, 18, 20, 22, 24, 26, 28, 30, 32, 34, 36

170 — Count by Threes!

MATH SKILLS

Count by threes

Write the missing numbers on the blocks.

3
6
9
12
15
18
21
24

171 — Count by Fours!

MATH SKILLS

Count by fours

Start at 4. Write the missing numbers on the cars.

40, 4, 36, 8, 32, 12, 28, 16, 24, 20

If there were 4 more cars on the Ferris wheel, what number would be on the last car?

56

172 — Count by Fives!

MATH SKILLS

Count by fives

Write the missing numbers on the flags.

5, 10, 15, 20, 25, 30, 35

40, 45, 50, 55, 60, 65, 70

75, 80, 85, 90, 95, 100

If the third row had 6 more flags, what number would be last? **130**

173 — Count by Tens!

MATH SKILLS

Count by tens

Write the missing numbers on the shirts.

10, 20, 30, 40, 50
60, 70, 80, 90, 100
110, 120, 130, 140, 150
160, 170, 180, 190, 200
210, 220, 230, 240, 250

174 — Count by Hundreds!

MATH SKILLS

Count by hundreds

Write the missing numbers on the suns.

100, 200, 300
400, 500, 600
700, 800, 900
1,000

176 — Addition in the Sky

ADDITION AND SUBTRACTION

Adding single-digit numbers

Add the numbers in each balloon.
If all the sums do not equal the number on the basket, cross out the balloon.

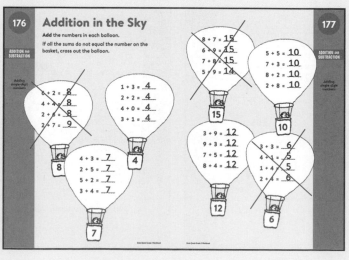

6 + 2 = 8
4 + 4 = 8
2 + 6 = 8
2 + 7 = ~~8~~
(crossed out) — 8

1 + 3 = 4
2 + 2 = 4
4 + 0 = 4
3 + 1 = 4
— 4

4 + 3 = 7
2 + 5 = 7
5 + 2 = 7
3 + 4 = 7
— 7

177

ADDITION AND SUBTRACTION

Adding single-digit numbers

8 + 7 = 15
6 + 9 = 15
7 + 8 = 15
5 + 9 = 14
(crossed out) — 15

5 + 5 = 10
7 + 3 = 10
8 + 2 = 10
2 + 8 = 10
— 10

3 + 9 = 12
9 + 3 = 12
7 + 5 = 12
8 + 4 = 12
— 12

3 + 3 = 6
4 + 1 = 5
1 + 4 = 5
2 + 4 = 6
(crossed out) — 6

Brain Quest Grade 2 Workbook

178 — Go Fish!

Finish the **fact families**. Write the missing numbers.

11
$4 + 7 = 11$
$7 + 4 = 11$
$11 - 4 = 7$
$11 - 7 = 4$

15
$9 + 6 = 15$
$6 + 9 = 15$
$15 - 9 = 6$
$15 - 6 = 9$

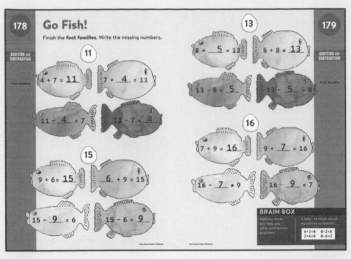

179

13
$8 + 5 = 13$
$5 + 8 = 13$
$13 - 8 = 5$
$13 - 5 = 8$

16
$7 + 9 = 16$
$9 + 7 = 16$
$16 - 7 = 9$
$16 - 9 = 7$

BRAIN BOX
Addition facts can help you solve subtraction problems.

It helps to think about equations as families:
$6 + 2 = 8$ $8 - 2 = 6$
$2 + 6 = 8$ $8 - 6 = 2$

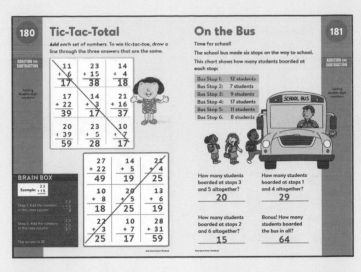

180 — Tic-Tac-Total

Add each set of numbers. To win tic-tac-toe, draw a line through the three answers that are the same.

11 + 6 = 17	23 + 15 = 38	14 + 4 = 18
17 + 22 = 39	14 + 17 = 31	21 + 16 = 37
20 + 39 = 59	23 + 5 = 28	10 + 7 = 17

27 + 22 = 49	14 + 5 = 19	21 + 4 = 25
10 + 8 = 18	20 + 5 = 25	13 + 6 = 19
22 + 3 = 25	10 + 7 = 17	28 + 31 = 59

BRAIN BOX
Example: 22 + 15

Step 1: Add the numbers in the ones column.

Step 2: Add the numbers in the tens column.

The answer is 37.

181 — On the Bus

Time for school!

The school bus made six stops on the way to school. This chart shows how many students boarded at each stop:

Bus Stop 1:	12 students
Bus Stop 2:	7 students
Bus Stop 3:	9 students
Bus Stop 4:	17 students
Bus Stop 5:	11 students
Bus Stop 6:	8 students

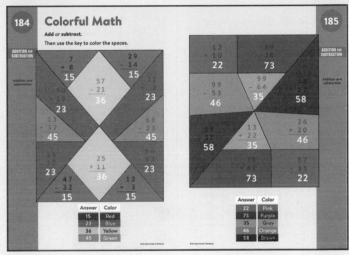

How many students boarded at stops 3 and 5 altogether?
20

How many students boarded at stops 1 and 4 altogether?
29

How many students boarded at stops 2 and 6 altogether?
15

Bonus! How many students boarded the bus in all?
64

182 — Tic-SubTract-Toe

Subtract the numbers. To win tic-tac-toe, draw a line through the three answers that are the same.

19 − 5 = 14	25 − 4 = 21	38 − 26 = 12
15 − 2 = 13	26 − 13 = 13	28 − 15 = 13
27 − 5 = 22	28 − 11 = 17	30 − 10 = 20

21 − 10 = 11	28 − 2 = 26	18 − 4 = 14
29 − 11 = 18	15 − 4 = 11	31 − 21 = 10
25 − 20 = 5	27 − 1 = 26	23 − 12 = 11

BRAIN BOX
Example: 26 − 12

Step 1: Subtract the numbers in the ones column.

Step 2: Subtract the numbers in the tens column.

The answer is 14.

183 — Camping Trip!

Subtract to solve the problems.

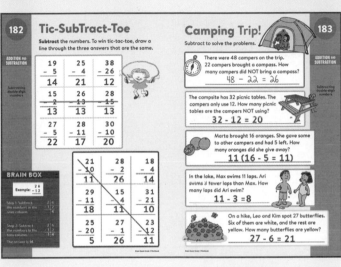

There were 48 campers on the trip. 22 campers brought a compass. How many campers did NOT bring a compass?
$48 − 22 = 26$

The campsite has 32 picnic tables. The campers only use 12. How many picnic tables are the campers NOT using?
$32 − 12 = 20$

Marta brought 16 oranges. She gave some to other campers and had 5 left. How many oranges did she give away?
$11 \ (16 − 5 = 11)$

In the lake, Max swims 11 laps. Ari swims 3 fewer laps than Max. How many laps did Ari swim?
$11 − 3 = 8$

On a hike, Leo and Kim spot 27 butterflies. Six of them are white, and the rest are yellow. How many butterflies are yellow?
$27 − 6 = 21$

184 — Colorful Math

Add or subtract.
Then use the key to color the spaces.

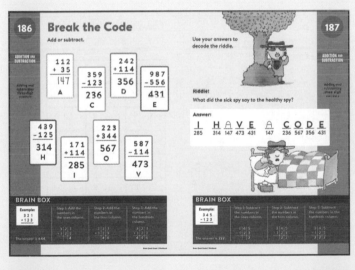

$7 + 8 = 15$
$29 − 14 = 15$
$57 − 21 = 36$
$25 + 11 = 36$
23, 45, 68, 15 ...

Answer	Color
15	Red
23	Blue
36	Yellow
45	Green

185

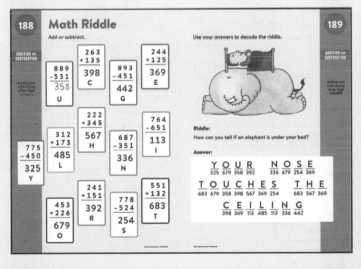

$12 + 10 = 22$
$87 − 16 = 73$
$99 − 53 = 46$
$99 − 64 = 35$
$13 + 22 = 35$
$26 + 20 = 46$
58, 22, 73 ...

Answer	Color
22	Pink
73	Purple
35	Gray
46	Orange
58	Brown

186 — Break the Code

Add or subtract.

$112 + 35 = 147$ **A**
$359 − 123 = 236$ **C**
$242 + 114 = 356$ **D**
$987 − 556 = 431$ **E**
$439 − 125 = 314$ **H**
$171 + 114 = 285$ **O**
$223 + 344 = 567$ **O**
$587 − 114 = 473$ **V**

BRAIN BOX
Example: 321 + 123

Step 1: Add the numbers in the ones column.

Step 2: Add the numbers in the tens column.

Step 3: Add the numbers in the hundreds column.

The answer is 444.

187

Use your answers to decode the riddle.

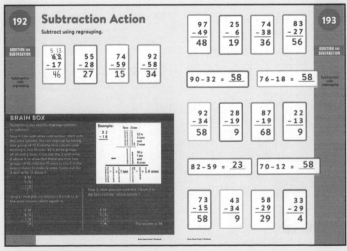

Riddle:
What did the sick spy say to the healthy spy?

Answer:
I HAVE A CODE
285 314 147 473 431 147 236 567 356 431

BRAIN BOX
Example: 345 − 123

Step 1: Subtract the numbers in the ones column.

Step 2: Subtract the numbers in the tens column.

Step 3: Subtract the numbers in the hundreds column.

The answer is 222.

188 — Math Riddle

Add or subtract.

$889 − 531 = 358$ **U**
$263 + 135 = 398$ **C**
$893 − 451 = 442$ **G**
$244 + 125 = 369$ **E**
$222 + 345 = 567$
$764 − 651 = 113$ **I**
$312 + 173 = 485$ **L**
$687 − 351 = 336$ **N**
$775 − 450 = 325$ **Y**
$241 + 151 = 392$ **R**
$778 − 524 = 254$ **S**
$551 + 132 = 683$ **T**
$453 + 226 = 679$ **O**

189

Use your answers to decode the riddle.

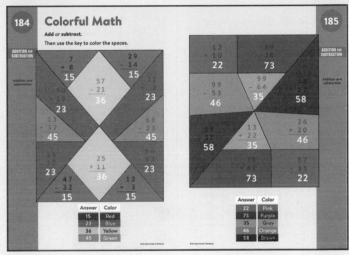

Riddle:
How can you tell if an elephant is under your bed?

Answer:
YOUR NOSE
325 679 358 392   336 679 254 369

TOUCHES THE
683 679 398 567 369 254   683 567 369

CEILING
398 369 113 485 113 336 442

190 — Math Pun

Add using regrouping.

$38 + 8 = 46$ **A**
$15 + 38 = 53$ **S**
$54 + 18 = 72$ **T**
$31 + 19 = 50$ **I**
$26 + 9 = 35$ **B**
$25 + 16 = 41$ **N**
$58 + 26 = 84$ **K**

BRAIN BOX
Sometimes you need to regroup numbers when you add. Regrouping means to rearrange a number according to its place value to make it easier to work with.

191

23 + 69 = 92 **L**	68 + 19 = 87 **O**	77 + 17 = 94 **R**	38 + 29 = 67 **G**

Use your answers to decode the riddle.

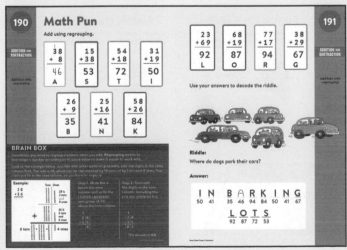

Riddle:
Where do dogs park their cars?

Answer:
IN BARKING
50 41   35 46 94 84 50 41

LOTS
92 87 72 53

192 — Subtraction Action

Subtract using regrouping.

$63 − 17 = 46$
$55 − 28 = 27$
$74 − 59 = 15$
$92 − 58 = 34$

BRAIN BOX
Sometimes you need to regroup numbers to subtract.

193

97 − 49 = 48	25 − 6 = 19	74 − 38 = 36	83 − 27 = 56

$90 − 32 = 58$
$76 − 18 = 58$

92 − 34 = 58	28 − 19 = 9	87 − 19 = 68	22 − 13 = 9

$82 − 59 = 23$
$70 − 12 = 58$

73 − 15 = 58	43 − 34 = 9	58 − 29 = 29	33 − 29 = 4

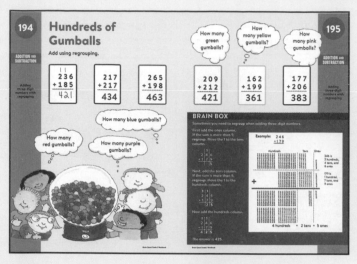

194 Hundreds of Gumballs

Add using regrouping.

$$236 + 185 = 421$$
$$217 + 217 = 434$$
$$265 + 198 = 463$$

195

How many green gumballs?
$$209 + 212 = 421$$

How many yellow gumballs?
$$162 + 199 = 361$$

How many pink gumballs?
$$177 + 206 = 383$$

How many blue gumballs?
How many purple gumballs?
How many red gumballs?

BRAIN BOX

Sometimes you need to regroup when adding three-digit numbers.

First add the ones column. If the sum is more than 9, regroup. Move the 1 to the tens column.

Next, add the tens column. If the sum is more than 9, regroup. Move the 1 to the hundreds column.

Now add the hundreds column.

Example: $246 + 179$

246 is 2 hundreds, 4 tens, and 6 ones.
179 is 1 hundred, 7 tens, and 9 ones.

4 hundreds + 2 tens + 5 ones

The answer is 425.

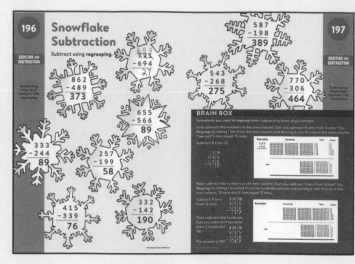

196 Snowflake Subtraction

Subtract using regrouping.

$$721 - 694 = 27$$
$$862 - 489 = 373$$
$$655 - 566 = 89$$
$$333 - 244 = 89$$
$$257 - 199 = 58$$
$$415 - 339 = 76$$
$$332 - 142 = 190$$

197

$$587 - 198 = 389$$
$$543 - 268 = 275$$
$$770 - 306 = 464$$

BRAIN BOX

Sometimes you need to regroup when subtracting three-digit numbers.

First subtract the numbers in the ones column. Can you subtract 8 ones from 5 ones? No. Regroup by taking 1 ten from the tens column and turning it into 10 ones in the ones column. 1 ten and 5 ones equal 15 ones.

Subtract 8 from 15.

Next subtract the numbers in the tens column. Can you subtract 9 tens from 3 tens? No. Regroup by taking 1 hundred from the hundreds column and turning it into 10 tens in the tens column. 10 tens and 2 tens equal 12 tens.

Subtract 9 tens from 12 tens.

Then subtract the hundreds. Can you subtract 1 hundred from 2 hundreds? Yes.

The answer is 137.

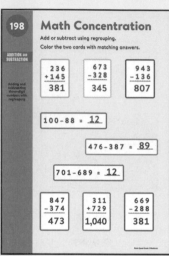

198 Math Concentration

Add or subtract using regrouping. Color the two cards with matching answers.

$$236 + 145 = 381$$
$$673 - 328 = 345$$
$$943 - 136 = 807$$
$$100 - 88 = 12$$
$$476 - 387 = 89$$
$$701 - 689 = 12$$
$$847 - 374 = 473$$
$$311 + 729 = 1{,}040$$
$$669 - 288 = 381$$

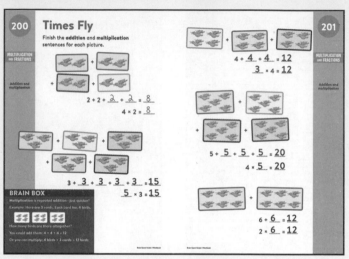

200 Times Fly

Finish the **addition** and **multiplication** sentences for each picture.

$$2 + 2 + 2 + 2 = 8$$
$$4 \times 2 = 8$$

$$3 + 3 + 3 + 3 + 3 = 15$$
$$5 \times 3 = 15$$

201

$$4 + 4 + 4 = 12$$
$$3 \times 4 = 12$$

$$5 + 5 + 5 + 5 = 20$$
$$4 \times 5 = 20$$

$$6 + 6 = 12$$
$$2 \times 6 = 12$$

BRAIN BOX

Multiplication is repeated addition—just quicker!

Example: Here are 3 cards. Each card has 4 birds.

How many birds are there altogether?
You could add them: $4 + 4 + 4 = 12$
Or you can multiply: 4 birds × 3 cards = 12 birds

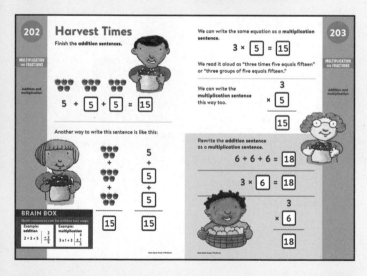

202 Harvest Times

Finish the **addition** sentences.

$$5 + 5 + 5 = 15$$

Another way to write this sentence is like this:

$$5 + 5 + 5 + 5 = 15$$ (15, 15)

BRAIN BOX

Math sentences can be written two ways.

Example: addition $2 + 3 = 5$
Example: multiplication $3 \times 1 = 3$

203

We can write the same equation as a multiplication sentence.

$$3 \times 5 = 15$$

We read it aloud as "three times five equals fifteen" or "three groups of five equals fifteen."

We can write the multiplication sentence this way too.

$$\begin{array}{r} 3 \\ \times 5 \\ \hline 15 \end{array}$$

Rewrite the addition sentence as a multiplication sentence.

$$6 + 6 + 6 = 18$$
$$3 \times 6 = 18$$
$$\begin{array}{r} 3 \\ \times 6 \\ \hline 18 \end{array}$$

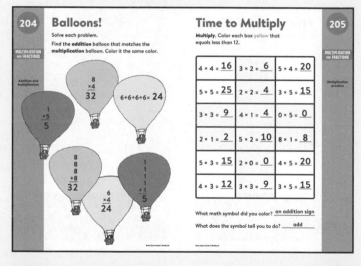

204 Balloons!

Solve each problem. Find the **addition** balloon that matches the **multiplication** balloon. Color it the same color.

$$\begin{array}{r} 8 \\ \times 4 \\ \hline 32 \end{array}$$
$$6 + 6 + 6 + 6 = 24$$
$$\begin{array}{r} 1 \\ \times 5 \\ \hline 5 \end{array}$$
$$8 + 8 + 8 + 8 = 32$$
$$\begin{array}{r} 6 \\ \times 4 \\ \hline 24 \end{array}$$
$$1 + 1 + 1 + 1 + 1 = 5$$

205 Time to Multiply

Multiply. Color each box yellow that equals less than 12.

$4 \times 4 = 16$	$3 \times 2 = 6$	$5 \times 4 = 20$
$5 \times 5 = 25$	$2 \times 2 = 4$	$3 \times 5 = 15$
$3 \times 3 = 9$	$4 \times 1 = 4$	$0 \times 5 = 0$
$2 \times 1 = 2$	$5 \times 2 = 10$	$8 \times 1 = 8$
$5 \times 3 = 15$	$2 \times 0 = 0$	$4 \times 5 = 20$
$4 \times 3 = 12$	$3 \times 3 = 9$	$3 \times 5 = 15$

What math symbol did you color? an addition sign

What does the symbol tell you to do? add

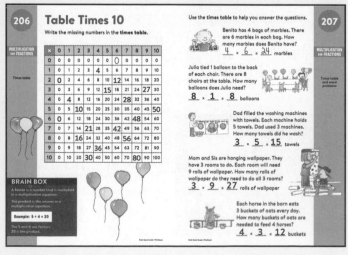

206 Table Times 10

Write the missing numbers in the **times table**.

×	0	1	2	3	4	5	6	7	8	9	10
0	0	0	0	0	0	0	0	0	0	0	0
1	0	1	2	3	4	5	6	7	8	9	10
2	0	2	4	6	8	10	12	14	16	18	20
3	0	3	6	9	12	15	18	21	24	27	30
4	0	4	8	12	16	20	24	28	32	36	40
5	0	5	10	15	20	25	30	35	40	45	50
6	0	6	12	18	24	30	36	42	48	54	60
7	0	7	14	21	28	35	42	49	56	63	70
8	0	8	16	24	32	40	48	56	64	72	80
9	0	9	18	27	36	45	54	63	72	81	90
10	0	10	20	30	40	50	60	70	80	90	100

BRAIN BOX

A factor is a number that is multiplied in a multiplication equation.

The product is the answer in a multiplication equation.

Example: $5 \times 4 = 20$

The 5 and 4 are factors.
20 is the product.

207

Use the times table to help you answer the questions.

Benito has 4 bags of marbles. There are 6 marbles in each bag. How many marbles does Benito have?
$$4 \times 6 = 24 \text{ marbles}$$

Julia tied 1 balloon to the back of each chair. There are 8 chairs at the table. How many balloons does Julia need?
$$8 \times 1 = 8 \text{ balloons}$$

Dad filled the washing machines with towels. Each machine holds 5 towels. Dad used 3 machines. How many towels did he wash?
$$3 \times 5 = 15 \text{ towels}$$

Mom and Sis are hanging wallpaper. They have 3 rooms to do. Each room will need 9 rolls of wallpaper. How many rolls of wallpaper do they need to do all 3 rooms?
$$3 \times 9 = 27 \text{ rolls of wallpaper}$$

Each horse in the barn eats 3 buckets of oats every day. How many buckets of oats are needed to feed 4 horses?
$$4 \times 3 = 12 \text{ buckets}$$

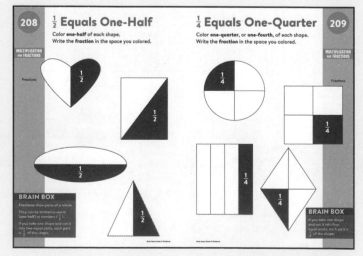

208 ½ Equals One-Half

Color **one-half** of each shape. Write the **fraction** in the space you colored.

$\frac{1}{2}$ (heart)
$\frac{1}{2}$ (square)
$\frac{1}{2}$ (oval)
$\frac{1}{2}$ (triangle)

BRAIN BOX

Fractions show parts of a whole.

They can be written as words. (one-half) or numbers ($\frac{1}{2}$).

If you take one shape and cut it into two equal parts, each part is $\frac{1}{2}$ of the shape.

209 ¼ Equals One-Quarter

Color **one-quarter**, or **one-fourth**, of each shape. Write the **fraction** in the space you colored.

$\frac{1}{4}$ (circle)
$\frac{1}{4}$ (square)
$\frac{1}{4}$ (diamond)

BRAIN BOX

If you take one shape and cut it into four equal parts, each part is $\frac{1}{4}$ of the shape.

⅓ Equals One-Third

Color **one-third** of each shape.
Write the **fraction** in the space you colored.

Fractions

BRAIN BOX
If you take one shape and cut it into three equal parts, each part is ⅓ of the shape.

A Piece of Pie

Draw a line from the **fraction** to the matching shape.

Matching fractions

½   ¼   ⅓   2/4

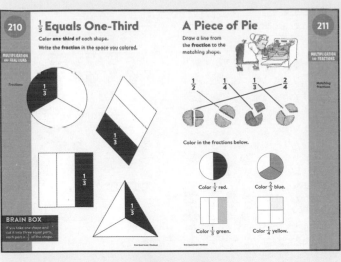

Color in the fractions below.

Color ½ red.   Color ⅔ blue.

Color ⅓ green.   Color ¼ yellow.

Word Problems

Read each problem.
Write the answer in **words** on the line.
Write the answer as a **fraction** in the box.

Ian cut his muffin in half. If he eats half of the muffin, how much will he have left to give to his little brother?

one half | ½ |

Fred's dog Daisy just had three puppies! One puppy is pure black. The other two are brown with little black spots. What fraction of the puppies are spotted?

two thirds | ⅔ |

Dolores picked three yellow flowers and one pink flower. What fraction of the flowers are pink?

one fourth | ¼ |

Name That Shape!

Read the clues.
Write the names of the shapes.

I have four sides. Two of my sides are short. Two are long.
What am I? _rectangle_

I have no sides at all. I go round and round.
What am I? _circle_

I have four sides. Each side is the same length.
What am I? _square_

I have four sides. You can find me in a deck of cards or on a baseball field.
What am I? _diamond_

I have three sides.
What am I? _triangle_

Same Shape

Look at the shape on the top card.
Draw a matching shape on the card below.

Geometry Mystery

Read the clues.
Write the names of the shapes.

cube   cone   pyramid   box   sphere

I have a round bottom and a pointed top.
What am I? _cone_

I am round all over.
What am I? _sphere_

I have four rectangular sides. I have two sides that are square.
What am I? _box_

I have a square base and a pointed top.
What am I? _pyramid_

I have six square sides.
What am I? _cube_

Made to Measure

Choose the correct word from the boxes below to complete each sentence.

weight   length
volume   temperature

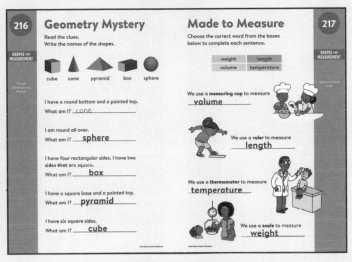

We use a **measuring cup** to measure
volume

We use a **ruler** to measure
length

We use a **thermometer** to measure
temperature

We use a **scale** to measure
weight

Measure It!

Write the **weight** of each basket of fruit.
Then answer the questions.

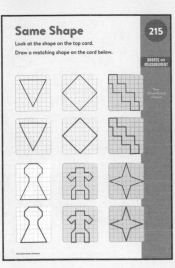

_7_ pounds   _4_ pounds

To measure the water in a bathtub, would you use a **cup** or a **gallon jug**?
a gallon jug

To measure the distance from your room to the kitchen, would you use **feet** or **miles**?
feet

If the thermometer reads 35°F, would you wear a **swimsuit** or a **snowsuit**?
a snowsuit

Inch by Inch

Cut out the **ruler** along the dotted line.
Use it to measure the pictures.
Then complete the sentences.
Save your ruler to use for the next four pages.

The quarter is _1_ inch wide.

The teaspoon is _5_ inches long.

The toy car is _3_ inches long.

The key is _1½_ inches long.

BRAIN BOX
To use your Brain Quest ruler, put the red short edge at one end of the object you want to measure.
See where the end of the object lines up with the ruler. That number is your final measurement.

What Time Is It?

Find the two clocks that match the words.
Draw lines between the words and the matching clocks.

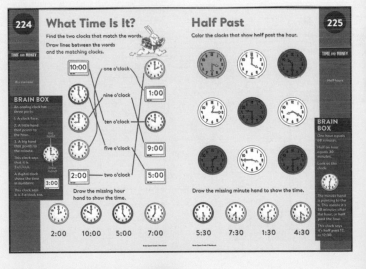

10:00   one o'clock
        nine o'clock   1:00
        ten o'clock
        five o'clock   9:00
2:00   two o'clock   5:00
3:00

Draw the missing hour hand to show the time.

2:00   10:00   5:00   7:00

BRAIN BOX
An analog clock has three parts:
1. A clock face.
2. A little hand that points to the hour.
3. A big hand that points to the minute.
This clock says that it is 3 o'clock.
A digital clock shows the time in numbers.
This clock says it is 3 o'clock too.

Half Past

Color the clocks that show half past the hour.

Draw the missing minute hand to show the time.

5:30   7:30   1:30   4:30

BRAIN BOX
One hour equals 60 minutes.
Half an hour equals 30 minutes.
Look at this clock.
The minute hand is pointing to the 6. This means it is 30 minutes after the hour, or half past the hour.
This clock says it's half past 12, or 12:30.

15 Minutes Before and After

Find the clock faces that show a **quarter past** the hour. Color them yellow.

Find the clock faces that show a **quarter to** the hour. Color them blue.

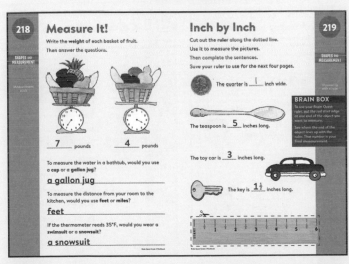

BRAIN BOX
A quarter hour is 15 minutes.
Look at this clock:
The minute hand is pointing to the 3. This means it's 15 minutes after the hour, or a quarter past.
The clock says it's a quarter past 1 or 1:15.
Now look at this clock:
The minute hand is pointing to the 9. This means it's 45 minutes after the hour, or 1:45. It also means that it is 15 minutes to the next hour, or a quarter to 2:00.

Draw the missing minute hand to show the time.

12:15   11:45   5:45   8:15

It's Getting Late!

Draw the minute hand to show the time on the hour.
Write the missing times on the lines.

1:00   _2:00_   3:00   _4:00_

5:00   _6:00_   7:00   _8:00_

What time is it right now?
Write the time on the line.
Draw the clock hands.

What time will it be in an hour?
Write the time on the line.
Draw the clock hands.

Tell the Time

Write the time below each clock.

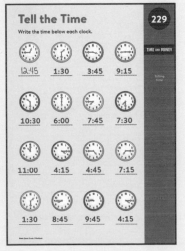

_12:45_   1:30   3:45   9:15

10:30   6:00   7:45   7:30

11:00   4:15   4:45   7:15

1:30   8:45   9:45   4:15

Money Riddles

Read the clues and questions.
Circle the answers.

TIME AND MONEY

Penny, nickel, dime, quarter

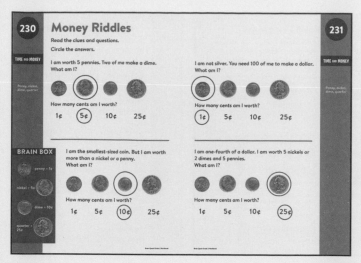

I am worth 5 pennies. Two of me make a dime.
What am I?

How many cents am I worth?

1¢   (5¢)   10¢   25¢

I am not silver. You need 100 of me to make a dollar.
What am I?

How many cents am I worth?

(1¢)   5¢   10¢   25¢

BRAIN BOX

penny = 1¢
nickel = 5¢
dime = 10¢
quarter = 25¢

I am the smallest-sized coin. But I am worth more than a nickel or a penny.
What am I?

How many cents am I worth?

1¢   5¢   (10¢)   25¢

I am one-fourth of a dollar. I am worth 5 nickels or 2 dimes and 5 pennies.
What am I?

How many cents am I worth?

1¢   5¢   10¢   (25¢)

TIME AND MONEY

Penny, nickel, dime, quarter

Fruit Stand

Circle the exact change needed to buy each fruit.
Then count the change left over.

TIME AND MONEY

Counting money

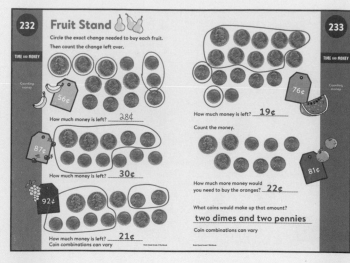

56¢

How much money is left? 28¢

87¢

How much money is left? 30¢

92¢

How much money is left? 21¢
Coin combinations can vary

TIME AND MONEY

Counting money

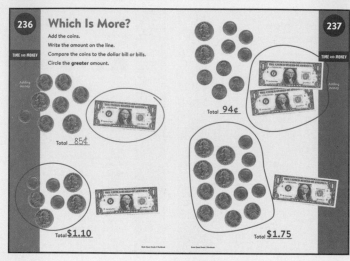

76¢

How much money is left? 19¢

Count the money.

How much more money would you need to buy the oranges? 22¢

81¢

What coins would make up that amount?

two dimes and two pennies

Coin combinations can vary

Got Change?

How many of each coin equal a **dollar**?
Write the missing numbers in the chart.

TIME AND MONEY

Change for a dollar

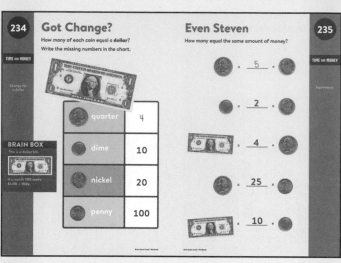

quarter	4
dime	10
nickel	20
penny	100

BRAIN BOX

This is a dollar bill.

It is worth 100 cents.
$1.00 = 100¢

Even Steven

How many equal the same amount of money?

TIME AND MONEY

Equivalents

__5__ ×

__2__ ×

__4__ ×

__25__ ×

__10__ ×

Which Is More?

Add the coins.
Write the amount on the line.
Compare the coins to the dollar bill or bills.
Circle the **greater** amount.

TIME AND MONEY

Adding money

Total __85¢__

Total __$1.10__

TIME AND MONEY

Adding money

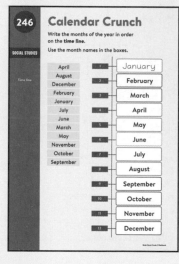

Total 94¢

Total __$1.75__

Map It!

Use the **map key** to label the continents.

SOCIAL STUDIES

Reading a map

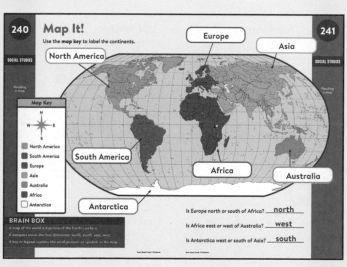

Europe

Asia

North America

Map Key

N W S E

North America
South America
Europe
Asia
Australia
Africa
Antarctica

South America

Africa

Australia

Antarctica

BRAIN BOX

A map of the world is a picture of the Earth's surface.
A compass shows the four directions: north, south, east, west.
A key or legend explains the small pictures or symbols on the map.

SOCIAL STUDIES

Reading a map

Is Europe north or south of Africa? __north__

Is Africa east or west of Australia? __west__

Is Antarctica west or south of Asia? __south__

Following Directions

Use the **map** on the next page to complete the sentences.
All the kids start at school.

SOCIAL STUDIES

Map practice

I am going 4 blocks north and 1 block east.

Josh is going to the __music school__.

I am going 2 blocks south and 2 blocks west.

Jen is going to the __ball field__.

I am going 2 blocks south and 2 blocks east.

Jane is going to the __market__.

I am going 1 block north and 3 blocks east.

Jeremy is going to the __library__.

Calendar Crunch

Write the months of the year in order on the **time line**.
Use the month names in the boxes.

SOCIAL STUDIES

Time line

April
August
December
February
January
July
June
March
May
November
October
September

1	January
2	February
3	March
4	April
5	May
6	June
7	July
8	August
9	September
10	October
11	November
12	December

Transportation Time Line

Today, there are many ways to travel, but there were not as many options in the past. Read about the different kinds of transportation people have used over the years, then fill in the blanks on the time line.

SOCIAL STUDIES

Past, present, and future

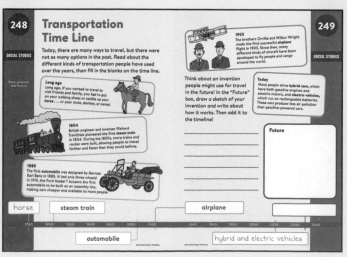

Long ago
Long ago, if you wanted to travel to visit friends and family, you had to put on your walking shoes or saddle up your horse ... or your mule, donkey, or camel.

1804
British engineer and inventor Richard Trevithick pioneered the first steam train in 1804. During the 1800s, more trains and routes were built, allowing people to travel farther and faster than they could before.

1885
The first automobile was designed by German Karl Benz in 1885. It had only three wheels! In 1915, the Ford Model T became the first automobile to be built on an assembly line, making cars cheaper and available to more people.

horse   steam train   automobile

SOCIAL STUDIES

1903
The brothers Orville and Wilbur Wright made the first successful **airplane** flight in 1903. Since then, many different kinds of aircraft have been developed to fly people and cargo around the world.

Think about an invention people might use for travel in the future! In the "Future" box, draw a sketch of your invention and write about how it works. Then add it to the timeline!

Today
Many people drive **hybrid cars**, which have both gasoline engines and electric motors, and **electric vehicles**, which run on rechargeable batteries. These cars produce less air pollution than gasoline-powered cars.

Future

airplane   hybrid and electric vehicles

SOCIAL STUDIES

Presidents' Day

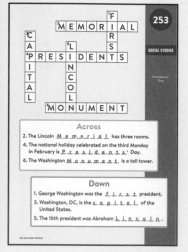

Across

2. The Lincoln M e m o r i a l has three rooms.
4. The national holiday celebrated on the third Monday in February is P r e s i d e n t s' Day.
6. The Washington M o n u m e n t is a tall tower.

Down

1. George Washington was the f i r s t president.
3. Washington, DC, is the c a p i t a l of the United States.
5. The 16th president was Abraham L i n c o l n.

Brain Quest Grade 2 Workbook

254 — Independence Day

SOCIAL STUDIES

Read about the Fourth of July.

We celebrate America's birthday on the fourth day of July. The Fourth of July is also called Independence Day.

On July 4, 1776, the Continental Congress met in Philadelphia, Pennsylvania, and adopted the Declaration of Independence. This paper said that America was no longer ruled by England. It declared America free! The Declaration is still a symbol of American liberty. We celebrate what it stands for every Fourth of July.

We celebrate this holiday in many different ways. To find out how, unscramble each word.

FIOKWERSR __fireworks__

LGAF __flag__

TCONREC __concert__

PRADEA __parade__

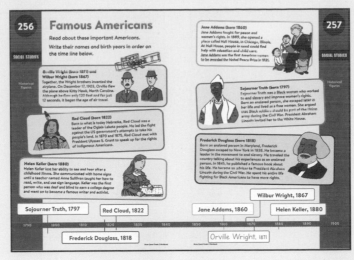

256 — Famous Americans

SOCIAL STUDIES

Read about these important Americans.

Write their names and birth years in order on the time line below.

Orville Wright (born 1871) and Wilbur Wright (born 1867)
Together, the Wright brothers invented the airplane. On December 17, 1903, Orville flew the plane above Kitty Hawk, North Carolina. Although the flight was only 120 feet and for just 12 seconds, it began the age of air travel.

Red Cloud (born 1822)
Born in what is today Nebraska, Red Cloud was a leader of the Oglala Lakota people. He led the fight against the US government's attempts to take his people's land. In 1870 and 1875, Red Cloud met with President Ulysses S. Grant to speak up for the rights of Indigenous Americans.

Helen Keller (born 1880)
Helen Keller lost her ability to see and hear after a childhood illness. She communicated with home signs until a teacher named Anne Sullivan taught her how to read, write, and use sign language. Keller was the first person who was deaf and blind to earn a college degree and went on to become a famous writer and activist.

257

SOCIAL STUDIES

Jane Addams (born 1860)
Jane Addams fought for peace and women's rights. In 1889, she opened a place called Hull House, in Chicago, Illinois. At Hull House, people in need could find help with education and child care. Jane Addams was the first American woman to be awarded the Nobel Peace Prize in 1931.

Sojourner Truth (born 1797)
Sojourner Truth was a Black woman who worked to end slavery and improve women's rights. Born an enslaved person, she escaped later in her life and lived as a free woman. She argued that Black children should be a part of the Union army during the Civil War. President Abraham Lincoln invited her to the White House.

Frederick Douglass (born 1818)
Born an enslaved person in Maryland, Frederick Douglass escaped to New York in 1838. He became a leader in the movement to end slavery. He traveled the country talking about his experiences as an enslaved person. In 1845, he published a famous book about his life. He became an adviser to President Abraham Lincoln during the Civil War. He spent his entire life fighting for Black Americans to have more rights.

| Sojourner Truth, 1797 | Red Cloud, 1822 | Jane Addams, 1860 | Helen Keller, 1880 |

Wilbur Wright, 1867

Frederick Douglass, 1818

Orville Wright, 1871

1790 1800 1810 1820 1830 1840 1850 1860 1870 1880 1890 1900

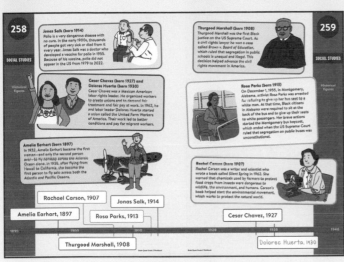

258

SOCIAL STUDIES

Jonas Salk (born 1914)
Polio is a very dangerous disease with no cure. In the early 1900s, thousands of people got very sick or died from it every year. Jonas Salk was a doctor who developed a vaccine for polio in 1955. Because of his vaccine, polio did not appear in the US from 1979 to 2022.

Cesar Chavez (born 1927) and Dolores Huerta (born 1930)
Cesar Chavez was a Mexican American labor rights leader. He organized workers to create unions and to demand fair treatment and fair pay at work. In 1962, he and labor leader Dolores Huerta started a union called the United Farm Workers of America. Their work led to better conditions and pay for migrant workers.

Amelia Earhart (born 1897)
In 1932, Amelia Earhart became the first woman—and only the second person ever—to fly nonstop across the Atlantic Ocean alone. In 1935, after flying from Hawaii to California, she became the first person to fly solo across both the Atlantic and Pacific Oceans.

Thurgood Marshall (born 1908)
Thurgood Marshall was the first Black justice on the US Supreme Court. As a civil rights lawyer he won a case called Brown v. Board of Education, which ruled that segregation in public schools is unequal and illegal. This decision helped advance the civil rights movement in America.

Rosa Parks (born 1913)
On December 1, 1955, in Montgomery, Alabama, activist Rosa Parks was arrested for refusing to give up her bus seat to a white man. At that time, Black citizens in Alabama were required to sit at the back of the bus and to give up their seats to white passengers. Her brave actions started the Montgomery bus boycott, which ended when the US Supreme Court ruled that segregation on public buses was unconstitutional.

Rachel Carson (born 1907)
Rachel Carson was a writer and scientist who wrote a book called Silent Spring in 1962. She warned that chemicals used by farmers to protect food crops from insects were dangerous to wildlife, the environment, and humans. Carson's book helped start the environmental movement, which works to protect the natural world.

259

SOCIAL STUDIES

Rachael Carson, 1907	Jonas Salk, 1914
Amelia Earhart, 1897	Rosa Parks, 1913	Cesar Chavez, 1927
Thurgood Marshall, 1908	Dolores Huerta, 1930

1890 1900 1910 1920 1930 1940

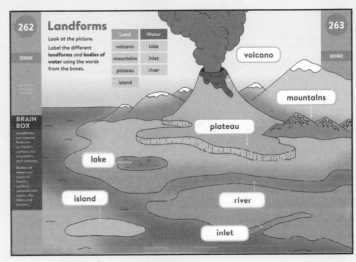

262 — Landforms

SCIENCE

Look at the picture. Label the different **landforms** and **bodies of water** using the words from the boxes.

Land	Water
volcano	lake
mountains	inlet
plateau	river
island	

BRAIN BOX
Landforms are natural features on Earth's surface, like mountains and canyons. Bodies of water are areas of Earth's surface covered with water, like lakes and oceans.

263

SCIENCE

volcano

mountains

plateau

lake

island

river

inlet

265

SCIENCE

Write **liquid**, **gas**, or **solid** under each picture.

solid — liquid

liquid — gas

solid — liquid

266 — Solid, Liquid, or Gas?

SCIENCE

Look at each picture. Is it showing a **solid**, a **liquid**, or a **gas**?

liquid — gas

solid — liquid

solid — liquid

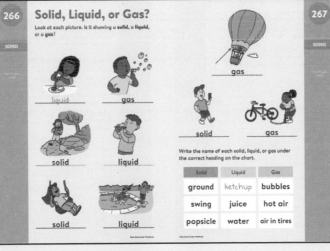

267

SCIENCE

gas

solid — gas

Write the name of each solid, liquid, or gas under the correct heading on the chart.

Solid	Liquid	Gas
ground	ketchup	bubbles
swing	juice	hot air
popsicle	water	air in tires

269

SCIENCE

Read about a photosynthesis experiment.

Number the pictures to show the correct order of the steps.

1. A plant uses sunlight to make food. A healthy plant is green.

2. Cover one leaf with foil.

3. After five days, uncover the leaf.

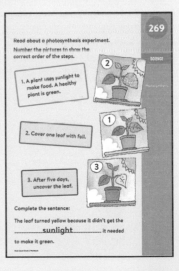

Complete the sentence:

The leaf turned yellow because it didn't get the _____ __sunlight__ _____ it needed to make it green.

270 — How Do Plants Grow?

SCIENCE

All plants need sunlight, water, and nutrients from soil to live and grow.

Where will a plant grow better? Circle your answer.

under a shady tree OR in direct sunlight?

in a rainy plain OR in a desert?

in soil with many nutrients OR in soil with no nutrients?

in a cave OR on a grassy hill?

on a glacier OR on a tropical island?

271 — Pollinating Plants

SCIENCE

Read the text below. Then answer the questions about **pollination**.

Pollinate means to move pollen from one plant to another. Bees, butterflies, birds, and other animals pollinate plants.

When an animal stops to feed at a flower, some of the flower's pollen grains stick to the animal. When the animal moves on to feed at another plant, it takes these pollen grains with it. This moves pollen around from plant to plant.

Wind and water can also pollinate by moving pollen grains from one plant to another.

Circle the correct answer. **Pollinate** means to:

Eat pollen grains | Move pollen grains from one plant to another | Fly by a plant quickly

Name two animals that are pollinators.

_____

Why do we need pollinators?

_____

BRAIN BOX
Pollen is powdery and found inside flowering plants. Pollen grains allow plants to reproduce, or make more plants.

272 — Address: Earth

SCIENCE

Read about **Earth** and circle it in the picture below.

You live in a home on a street or road.
Your street or road is in a town or city.
Your town or city is in a state.
Your state is in a country.
Your country is on a continent.
Your continent is on the planet Earth.
And where is Earth?

Earth is in the solar system. It is one of eight planets in our solar system that orbit (circle around) the sun. Pluto was once considered a planet, but scientists decided that it's too small to be considered a full planet. Pluto is now called a dwarf planet.

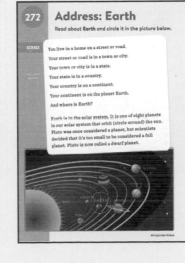

273

SCIENCE

Use the picture to answer the questions. List the eight planets that orbit the sun.

M __Mercury__
V __Venus__
E __Earth__
M __Mars__
J __Jupiter__
S __Saturn__
U __Uranus__
N __Neptune__

Which planet is closest to the sun?

__Mercury__

Which planet is farthest from the sun?

__Neptune__

Which two planets are Earth's closest neighbors?

__Venus and Mars__

BRAIN BOX
You can recall the order of the planets with a mnemonic (pronounced ni-mon-ik), a tool that helps you remember: My Very Excellent Mother Just Served Us Nachos.

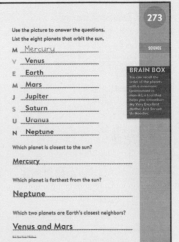

Stay Healthy!

SCIENCE

Maiko loves to jump rope to stay healthy.

She made a **chart** to keep track of how long she jumps rope each day.

Use her chart to answer the questions.

CHART

Day	Minutes
Mon.	15
Tues.	10
Wed.	20
Thurs.	12
Fri.	18
Sat.	18
Sun.	13

On which day did Maiko exercise the most?

Wednesday

On which day did she exercise the least?

Tuesday

On which two days did she exercise the same amount of time?

Friday and Saturday

SCIENCE

Use the chart to complete the **graph** for Thursday through Sunday. Color in each box until you reach the number of minutes for each day.

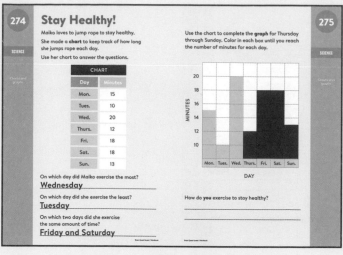

How do **you** exercise to stay healthy?

_____

Bird Riddles

SCIENCE

Draw a line from each bird riddle on this page to the correct bird on the next page.

My tail is so beautiful! I can fly, but I would rather walk and strut. What am I?

I have feathers and a beak, and I lay eggs like other birds. But I do not fly through the air. I fly through the water! What am I?

I am a beautiful bird too! I have a sharp beak. If you are patient, you might be able to teach me to say, "Polly want a cracker." What am I?

I am tall. I have a long neck. My feathers are pink from the pink shrimp I like to eat. What am I?

I am a small bird. The feathers on my chest are red. You see me in the spring. What am I?

I have a red comb on top of my head. In the early morning you might hear me call, "cock-a-doodle-do!" What am I?

SCIENCE

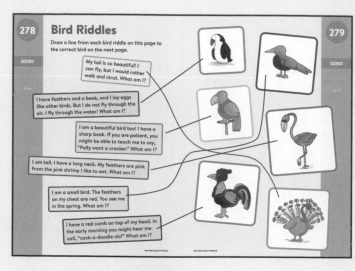

SCIENCE

Use words from below to complete the sentences.

Kenya   rough   oceans   years   fable

This story is not a f a b l e.

The waves were r o u g h.

Atlantic, Pacific, and Indian are names of

o c e a n s.

This happened in K e n y a.

A century is 100 y e a r s.

Write the letters from the colored boxes in the matching boxes below to complete the sentence.

Owen is one l u c k y hippo!

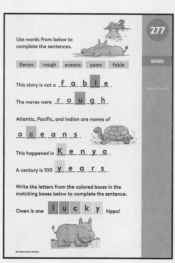

SCIENCE

The Camel's a Mammal

Read about **mammals**.

Mammals:
- breathe air through lungs.
- are born alive. They do not hatch.
- drink milk their mothers make.
- have hair. Some are born with hair and lose it as they grow up.

Circle all the mammals.

SCIENCE

Most mammals live on land, but some mammals live in the sea.

Sea mammals have lungs. They swim up to the surface to breathe air.

Sea creatures that are not mammals do not need to breathe air.

Circle the sea creatures that are mammals.

Icons!

TECHNOLOGY

Sometimes a small picture, called an **icon**, can tell us a lot of information. What happens if you click certain pictures on a computer? Draw a line between the icon and what it means or does.

word processor

paint program

cut text or pictures

go to a home page

close a program or window

turn power on or off

BRAIN BOX

Icons are little images, or pictures, that represent a program, an application, or an action that we can take on a computer or other digital device.

TECHNOLOGY

Which Key Am I?

Look at the computer keyboard. Find and color the key for each clue.

Color the key that will erase text blue.

Color the very long key that moves the cursor forward one space red.

Color the keys that make letters into capitals green.

Color the keys that make the computer sounds louder and softer purple.

Color the key that makes the cursor move to the beginning of the next row orange.

BRAIN BOX

A cursor is a shape that moves to show where you are working on a screen. It may look like an arrow that you can move with a mouse or trackpad, or it may look like a blinking line that shows where you will be typing.

TECHNOLOGY

Turtle Time!

A computer follows instructions called **commands**. Here are some commands you could use to make a robot move.

To move forward one step: MOVE FORWARD
To turn right: TURN RIGHT
To turn left: TURN LEFT

To make a robot move forward two steps and then turn right, you would write:

MOVE FORWARD
MOVE FORWARD
TURN RIGHT

Draw a path below to help the turtle robot reach the finish line. Remember to pay attention to the direction the turtle is facing!

START

FINISH   WRONG WAY!

TECHNOLOGY

Write the steps the turtle should take to reach the finish line. Remember to pay attention to the direction the turtle is facing. Hint: It should take ten steps!

MOVE FORWARD
TURN RIGHT
TURN LEFT

MOVE FORWARD
MOVE FORWARD
MOVE FORWARD
TURN RIGHT
MOVE FORWARD
MOVE FORWARD
TURN RIGHT
MOVE FORWARD
MOVE FORWARD

BRAIN BOX

Coders can use command blocks to write instructions for a computer. Coders begin with the step they want the computer to do first. The next step goes below the first. Coders continue writing steps until there is a complete list of directions for the computer to follow.

Loopy Loops!

TECHNOLOGY

Write a program to help the cat catch the mouse. Can you do it using just three commands?

Here are the commands you can use:

GO FORWARD 1
TURN RIGHT
LOOP [GO FORWARD 1] TIMES

START

BRAIN BOX

Programmers use loops to make their programs shorter. If you want to make a robot go forward 4 times, you can write:

Go forward 1,
Go forward 1,
Go forward 1,
Go forward 1,

Or you can use a loop by writing:

Loop [Go forward 1],
4 times

You can loop something any number of times!

Answer:

LOOP [GO FORWARD 1] 3 TIMES
TURN RIGHT
LOOP [GO FORWARD 1] 3 TIMES

TECHNOLOGY

A programmer's code can help the dog get to the bone, but three of the command blocks in the code below are NOT correct.

START

FINISH

Circle the mistakes, then write the correct steps.

Code	Correct steps
TURN RIGHT	TURN RIGHT
LOOP [GO FORWARD 1] 3 TIMES	LOOP [GO FORWARD 1] 3 TIMES
TURN LEFT	TURN LEFT
LOOP [GO FORWARD 1] 2 TIMES	
LOOP [GO FORWARD 1] 2 TIMES	TURN LEFT
TURN RIGHT	TURN LEFT
TURN LEFT	
GO FORWARD 1	TURN RIGHT
TURN RIGHT	
GO FORWARD 1	LOOP [GO FORWARD 1] 2 TIMES
	TURN RIGHT
	LOOP [GO FORWARD 1] 2 TIMES

TECHNOLOGY

This graph shows how many coins each bridge could hold.

Read the graph and answer the questions.

= 10 coins

Anton
Himari
Sybil

Did all the bridges support at least one coin? **yes**

How many coins did each bridge hold?

Anton	Himari	Sybil
30	80	50

Whose bridge held the most coins?

Himari

Whose bridge held the fewest coins?

Anton

Super Spy!

TECHNOLOGY

Before passwords, people used secret messages to keep their information private.

In this code, each letter of the alphabet has a number. What does the message say?

A	B	C	D	E	F	G	H	I	J
1	2	3	4	5	6	7	8	9	10

K	L	M	N	O	P	Q	R	S	T
11	12	13	14	15	16	17	18	19	20

U	V	W	X	Y	Z
21	22	23	24	25	26

Y O U   D I D   I T.
25 15 21   4 9 4   9 20

Can you write your name in code?

YOUR NAME IN LETTERS:

_____

YOUR NAME IN CODE (numbers):

_____

BRAIN BOX

Secret messages are a kind of encryption. Encryption is one way that computers keep your information private. Encrypting words or messages changes the text into a form that only a person with the password can read.

BRAIN QUEST EXTRAS

You did it! Time to make a Brain Quest Mini-Deck so you can play and learn wherever you go. Fill out your certificate and hang your poster. Great work!

PARENTS Congratulations to you and your child! In this section you can help your child cut out the Brain Quest Mini-Deck and certificate and hang up their poster. Continue to make learning part of your everyday life beyond this book. Find time to read aloud to your child each day, and keep asking questions to help encourage their curiosity and extend their learning.

For additional resources, visit www.BrainQuest.com/grade2

CONGRATULATIONS!

You've finished the Brain Quest Workbook!

All your hard work paid off! Ask a grown-up for help and cut out these SMART CARDS to make your own Brain Quest Mini-Deck.

You can play these anywhere—in the back of the car, at the park, or even at the grocery store. Remember: It's fun to be smart!

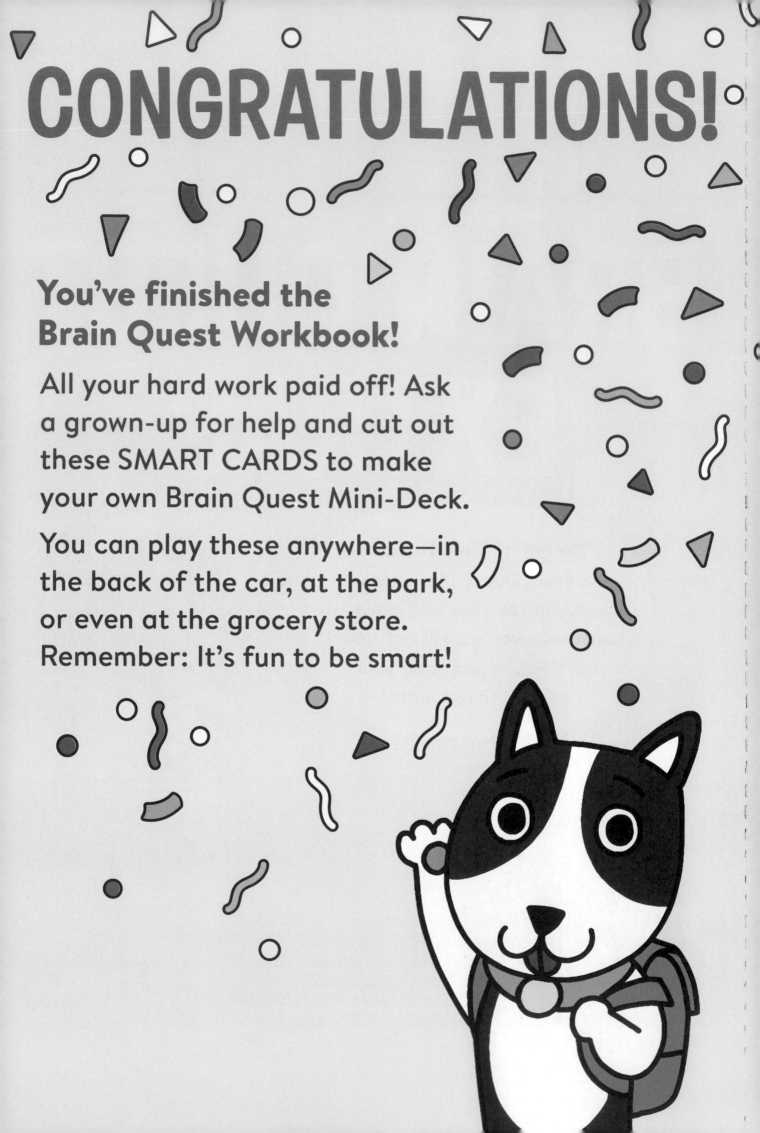

QUESTIONS

MATH 1 2 3 How many hundreds are in the number 839?

READING What's a shorter way to say "I am"?

MATH 1 2 3 Which is more: 4 pennies + 4 nickels or 2 dimes?

READING Find the verb in this sentence: "The red ball flew through the air."

BRAIN QUEST

QUESTIONS

MATH 1 2 3 Find the sum: 60 + 67.

READING If *d* and *r* are called consonants, what are *a* and *i* called?

MATH 1 2 3 My sister is 15 years old. How old will she be in 6 years?

READING How many beds does Goldilocks try?

BRAIN QUEST

QUESTIONS

MATH 1 2 3 Ariel drew a picture of 6 trees. Then she drew 3 flowers. How many plants did she draw in all?

LANGUAGE ARTS A B C Synonyms are words that have opposite meanings. True or false?

MATH 1 2 3 Which number doesn't belong here: 3, 7, 4, 9, 11?

READING Which word begins with an *s* sound: crispy, caterpillar, cereal, court?

BRAIN QUEST

QUESTIONS

MATH 1 2 3 Is the sum of 46 + 52 more or less than 100?

LANGUAGE ARTS A B C To find out the meaning of a word, do you use an atlas or a dictionary?

MATH 1 2 3 What do we call the total when numbers are added together?

READING Which is the correct spelling for a birthday dessert: c-a-k-e or c-a-c-k-e?

BRAIN QUEST

QUESTIONS

MATH 1 2 3 Pranith has 4 dimes, 3 nickels, and 1 penny. How much money does he have in all?

READING Find two synonyms: sad, polite, considerate, smiling.

MATH 1 2 3 Aurelia had 6 peaches. She gave 2 to her sister. How many peaches did Aurelia have left?

LANGUAGE ARTS A B C What's a longer way to say "haven't"?

BRAIN QUEST

QUESTIONS

MATH 1 2 3 Double 16. What number do you get?

LANGUAGE ARTS A B C Which spelling has an extra *r*: f-u-r-r-y, v-e-r-r-y, or h-u-r-r-y?

MATH 1 2 3 It's 7:30 a.m. What time will it be in 30 minutes?

READING Which word has a **hard** *c* sound: care or city?

BRAIN QUEST

Brain Quest Mini-Deck

ANSWERS

MATH 1 2 3

9 plants
(6 + 3 = 9)

LANGUAGE ARTS A B C

false (Synonyms are words that have similar meanings.)

MATH 1 2 3

4
(It is the only even number.)

READING

cereal

BRAIN QUEST®

ANSWERS

MATH 1 2 3

127

READING

vowels

MATH 1 2 3

21 years old
(15 + 6 = 21)

READING

three beds (too big, too small, and just right)

BRAIN QUEST®

ANSWERS

MATH 1 2 3

8 hundreds
(800 + 30 + 9 = 839)

READING

I'm

MATH 1 2 3

4 pennies + 4 nickels
(24¢ is more than 20¢.)

READING

"The red ball flew through the air."

BRAIN QUEST®

ANSWERS

MATH 1 2 3

32
(16 + 16 = 32)

LANGUAGE ARTS A B C

v-e-r-r-y
(The word is very.)

MATH 1 2 3

8:00 a.m.

READING

care

BRAIN QUEST®

ANSWERS

MATH 1 2 3

56¢
(40 + 15 + 1 = 56)

READING

polite, considerate

MATH 1 2 3

4 peaches (6 − 2 = 4)

LANGUAGE ARTS A B C

have not

BRAIN QUEST®

ANSWERS

MATH 1 2 3

less (98 < 100)

LANGUAGE ARTS A B C

a dictionary

MATH 1 2 3

the sum

READING

c-a-k-e (cake)

BRAIN QUEST®

Brain Quest Mini-Deck

QUESTIONS

 MATH 1 2 3 A decade is 10 years. How many years are in 7 decades?

 LANGUAGE ARTS A B C Find two words with the same meaning: small, soft, tiny, firm.

 MATH 1 2 3 What is the sum of 14 + 27?

 LANGUAGE ARTS A B C Which is correct: b–r–i–t–e or b–r–i–g–h–t?

BRAIN QUEST

QUESTIONS

 MATH 1 2 3 Margaret is 24 years old. Martin is half her age. How old is Martin?

 LANGUAGE ARTS A B C What is the word for more than one child?

 MATH 1 2 3 Is the number 4 worth more in 641 or in 416?

 LANGUAGE ARTS A B C Which of these is both a noun and a verb: place mat, napkin, bowl?

BRAIN QUEST

QUESTIONS

 MATH 1 2 3 I bought a sticker for 50¢ and socks for $2.00. How much did I spend in total?

 LANGUAGE ARTS A B C Put these colors in alphabetical order: red, blue, orange, green.

 MATH 1 2 3 Find the sum: 77 + 11.

 LANGUAGE ARTS A B C Which word has a different meaning than the others: large, big, loose, huge?

BRAIN QUEST

QUESTIONS

 MATH 1 2 3 Find the difference between 68 and 7.

 LANGUAGE ARTS A B C What word can you put in front of *coat* to name something you would wear in wet weather?

 MATH 1 2 3 How many quarters do you need to make $1.50?

 LANGUAGE ARTS A B C Spell the four-letter word that means the opposite of *empty*.

BRAIN QUEST

QUESTIONS

 MATH 1 2 3 My dog will be 14 in 5 years. How old is he now?

 LANGUAGE ARTS A B C Which word is both a noun and a verb: plant or trunk?

 MATH 1 2 3 What are the next two numbers in this pattern: 9, 7, 5, ___, ___?

 LANGUAGE ARTS A B C Find the antonyms in this group: back, below, behind, above.

BRAIN QUEST

QUESTIONS

 MATH 1 2 3 Mai wants to read 22 books. She has read 18. How many more does she need to reach her goal?

 LANGUAGE ARTS A B C To find out the story of someone's life, should you read a biography or an instruction manual?

 MATH 1 2 3 How many tens are in the number 341?

 LANGUAGE ARTS A B C Find the subject of this sentence: "Storms blew across the plains."

BRAIN QUEST

Brain Quest Mini-Deck

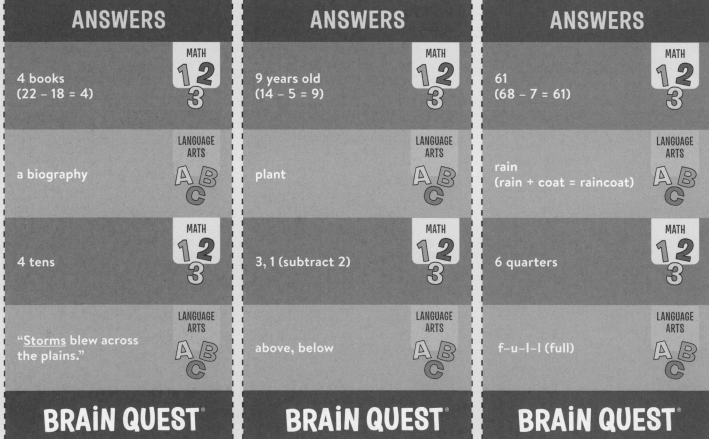

ANSWERS

MATH **1 2 3**

$2.50
(50¢ + 2.00 = 12.50)

LANGUAGE ARTS A B C

blue, green, orange, red

MATH **1 2 3**

88
(77 + 11 = 88)

LANGUAGE ARTS A B C

loose

BRAIN QUEST

ANSWERS

MATH **1 2 3**

12 years old
(½ of 24 is 12)

LANGUAGE ARTS A B C

children

MATH **1 2 3**

416 (The value of 4 in this number is 400.)

LANGUAGE ARTS A B C

bowl

BRAIN QUEST

ANSWERS

MATH **1 2 3**

70 years
(7 x 10 = 70)

LANGUAGE ARTS A B C

small, tiny

MATH **1 2 3**

41
(14 + 27 = 41)

LANGUAGE ARTS A B C

b–r–i–g–h–t (bright)

BRAIN QUEST

ANSWERS

MATH **1 2 3**

4 books
(22 – 18 = 4)

LANGUAGE ARTS A B C

a biography

MATH **1 2 3**

4 tens

LANGUAGE ARTS A B C

"Storms blew across the plains."

BRAIN QUEST

ANSWERS

MATH **1 2 3**

9 years old
(14 – 5 = 9)

LANGUAGE ARTS A B C

plant

MATH **1 2 3**

3, 1 (subtract 2)

LANGUAGE ARTS A B C

above, below

BRAIN QUEST

ANSWERS

MATH **1 2 3**

61
(68 – 7 = 61)

LANGUAGE ARTS A B C

rain
(rain + coat = raincoat)

MATH **1 2 3**

6 quarters

LANGUAGE ARTS A B C

f–u–l–l (full)

BRAIN QUEST

Brain Quest Mini-Deck

QUESTIONS

 MATH How many wheels does a tricycle have?

 READING Who wants to blow down the houses of the Three Little Pigs?

 MATH How much is 68 + 7?

 MISCELLANY Which should be written as one word: <u>sand box</u> or <u>sand dune</u>?

BRAIN QUEST®

QUESTIONS

 MATH If 4 + 3 equals 7, what does 4 + 3 + 3 equal?

 LANGUAGE ARTS What two letters must you put before a-g-o-n to spell the name of a fire-breathing creature?

 MATH Which doesn't measure length: an <u>inch</u>, a <u>pound</u>, a <u>centimeter</u>?

 READING The subject is one part of a sentence. What do we call the other part?

BRAIN QUEST®

QUESTIONS

 MATH How many tens and ones do you need to make 88?

 READING Put these words in alphabetical order: <u>seven</u>, <u>cup</u>, <u>book</u>, <u>mouth</u>.

 MATH What time is it when the hour hand is on the 3 and the minute hand is on the 12?

 LANGUAGE ARTS What's the word for more than one mouse?

BRAIN QUEST®

QUESTIONS

 MATH Ben needs 35 marbles. He has 18 blue ones and 15 green ones. Does he have enough?

 LANGUAGE ARTS Which word comes first in a dictionary: <u>mouse</u> or <u>giraffe</u>?

 MATH Which is greater: the <u>age of a second grader</u> or <u>the number of legs on a cat</u>?

 READING Which word is NOT a verb: <u>grow</u>, <u>sit</u>, <u>child</u>?

BRAIN QUEST®

QUESTIONS

 MATH Suki has 10 oranges. She gives 7 to her cousin. How many does she have left?

 LANGUAGE ARTS Rearrange the letters in the word *dam* to make another word for *angry*.

 MATH Which set of numbers does NOT add up to 12: <u>6 + 2 + 4</u> or <u>3 + 7 + 5</u>?

 LANGUAGE ARTS "Noah lent paper to Roberto and <u>I/me</u>." Which is correct?

BRAIN QUEST®

QUESTIONS

 MATH How do you write 5 + 5 + 5 as a multiplication problem?

 READING Which two words are antonyms: <u>small</u>, <u>slow</u>, <u>heavy</u>, <u>large</u>?

 MATH Find the shape of a postcard: <u>circle</u>, <u>oval</u>, <u>rectangle</u>.

 LANGUAGE ARTS "This is the <u>nicest/ most nice</u> shirt I own." Which is correct?

BRAIN QUEST®

Brain Quest Mini-Deck

ANSWERS

MATH 1 2 3
8 tens and 8 ones

READING
book, cup, mouth, seven

MATH 1 2 3
3:00

LANGUAGE ARTS A B C
mice

BRAIN QUEST

ANSWERS

MATH 1 2 3
10 (or 3 more than 7)

LANGUAGE ARTS A B C
d-r (dragon)

MATH 1 2 3
a pound

READING
the predicate

BRAIN QUEST

ANSWERS

MATH 1 2 3
3 (tri- means "three.")

READING
the Big Bad Wolf

MATH 1 2 3
75

MISCELLANY ?
sandbox

BRAIN QUEST

ANSWERS

MATH 1 2 3
3 × 5

READING
small, large

MATH 1 2 3
rectangle

LANGUAGE ARTS A B C
"This is the nicest shirt I own."

BRAIN QUEST

ANSWERS

MATH 1 2 3
3 oranges (10 − 7 = 3)

LANGUAGE ARTS A B C
mad

MATH 1 2 3
3 + 7 + 5 (equals 15)

LANGUAGE ARTS A B C
"Noah lent paper to Roberto and me."

BRAIN QUEST

ANSWERS

MATH 1 2 3
no (18 + 15 = 33)

LANGUAGE ARTS A B C
giraffe

MATH 1 2 3
the age of a second grader (A cat has 4 legs.)

READING
child

BRAIN QUEST

Brain Quest Mini-Deck

QUESTIONS

 MATH 1 2 3 Mercedes took 7 apples and 6 oranges. Daniel took 6 apples and 4 oranges. Who took more fruit?

 READING Which noun names a person: <u>classroom</u>, <u>teaching</u>, <u>teacher</u>?

 MATH 1 2 3 What is the sum of 12 + 13?

 READING Find a longer way to say "I'm feeling tired."

BRAIN QUEST

QUESTIONS

 MATH 1 2 3 What does the minus sign (–) tell you to do?

 LANGUAGE ARTS A B C Which word is spelled with one e: <u>bee</u> or <u>the</u>?

 MATH 1 2 3 It's 6:30. What time will it be in 1 hour?

 READING What's the opposite of *tall*?

BRAIN QUEST

QUESTIONS

 MATH 1 2 3 Which is longer: <u>1 minute</u> or <u>1 hour</u>?

 READING Which are rhyming words: <u>blue</u>, <u>do</u>, <u>show</u>?

 MATH 1 2 3 What three numbers come between 28 and 32?

 LANGUAGE ARTS A B C What is the fifth letter of the alphabet?

BRAIN QUEST

QUESTIONS

 MATH 1 2 3 How much is 834 – 100?

 READING Which is correct: "Abdul is taller than Josie" or "Abdul is more taller than Josie"?

 MATH 1 2 3 What is the sum of 24 + 13?

 READING What letter is missing from this synonym of *tiniest*: s-m-a-l-e-s-t?

BRAIN QUEST

QUESTIONS

 MATH 1 2 3 What is the largest three-digit number you can make with these digits: 4, 9, 7?

 READING Spell the word for the coin that's worth 10¢.

 MISCELLANY ? On a clock, how many minutes go by between the numbers 3 and 6?

 READING Find the opposite of *asleep*: <u>bed</u>, <u>awake</u>, <u>tired</u>, <u>dream</u>.

BRAIN QUEST

QUESTIONS

 MATH 1 2 3 4 + 9 = 7 + 6. True or false?

 LANGUAGE ARTS A B C Turn this sentence into a question: "Suri is coming over."

 MATH 1 2 3 Lee spent 2 dollars on a card and 4 dollars on ribbons. How much did she spend in all?

 LANGUAGE ARTS A B C What do we call two different words that sound the same?

BRAIN QUEST

Brain Quest Mini-Deck

ANSWERS

MATH 1 2 3

1 hour (There are 60 minutes in 1 hour.)

READING

blue, do

MATH 1 2 3

29, 30, 31

LANGUAGE ARTS A B C

E

BRAIN QUEST®

ANSWERS

MATH 1 2 3

subtract

LANGUAGE ARTS A B C

the

MATH 1 2 3

7:30

READING

short

BRAIN QUEST®

ANSWERS

MATH 1 2 3

Mercedes (7 + 6 = 13 and 6 + 4 = 10. 13 is more than 10.)

READING

teacher

MATH 1 2 3

25

READING

I am feeling tired.

BRAIN QUEST®

ANSWERS

MATH 1 2 3

true
(4 + 9 = 13; 7 + 6 = 13)

LANGUAGE ARTS A B C

"Is Suri coming over?"

MATH 1 2 3

6 dollars
($2 + $4 = $6)

LANGUAGE ARTS A B C

homophones

BRAIN QUEST®

ANSWERS

MATH 1 2 3

974

READING

d-i-m-e (dime)

MISCELLANY ?

15 minutes

READING

awake

BRAIN QUEST®

ANSWERS

MATH 1 2 3

734

READING

"Abdul is taller than Josie."

MATH 1 2 3

37

READING

I (The word is *smallest*.)

BRAIN QUEST®

YOU DID IT!

CONGRATULATIONS!

You completed every activity in the Brain Quest Grade 2 Workbook. Cut out the certificate (ask an adult for help!) and write your name on it. Show your friends! Hang it on the wall! You should feel proud of your hard work.

CERTIFICATE OF ACHIEVEMENT

Earned by

_____

for completing all sections in the

BRAIN QUEST®
GRADE 2 WORKBOOK